Moon Method Diary 2025

Created by Anna Maria Whitehead

© COPYRIGHT ANNA MARIA WHITEHEAD 2025

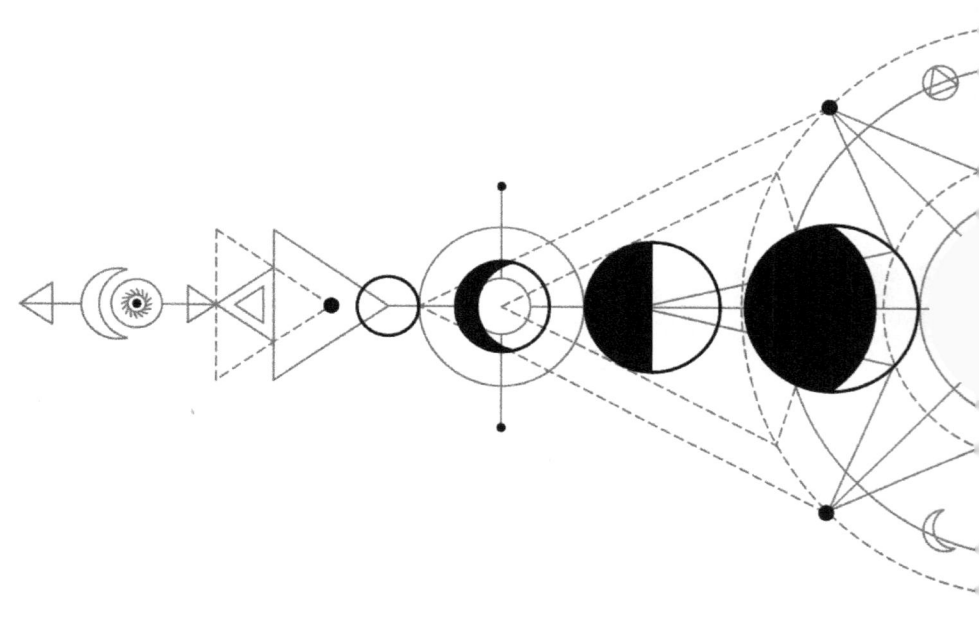

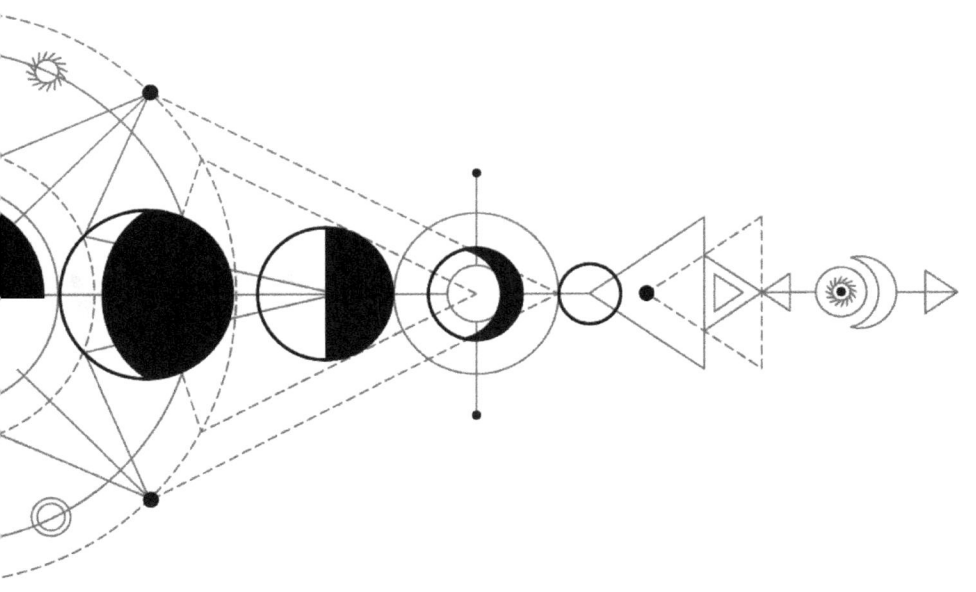

LUNAR CALENDAR 2025

Great Mystery,
Teach me how to trust
my heart,
my mind,
my intuition,
my inner knowing,
the senses of my body,
the blessings of my spirit.
Teach me to trust these things
so that I may enter my Sacred Space
and love beyond my fear,
and thus Walk in Balance
with the passing of each glorious Sun
 - Lakota Prayer.

Phases of the moon

New Moon
New beginnings and intention setting. Listen to your intuition.

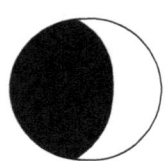
Waxing Moon
Put plans into action

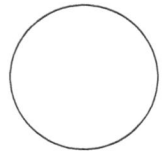
Full Moon
Gratitude for all you have received. Tune in to your heart to discover what you need to release during the waning moon.

Waning Moon
Release anything that no longer serves you

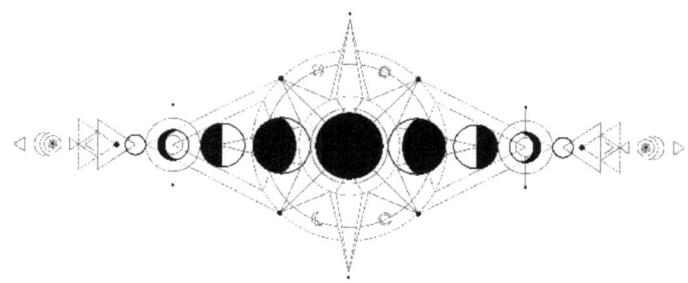

Working with the moon

Live in sync with nature to manifest your best life.

Do you ever feel overwhelmed with to-do lists? Do you experience days when you have planned to see a friend, only to find when the day comes along you do not feel like socialising?

The secret is being able to forward plan our schedules by having an idea of where our energy levels will be at different times throughout the month. Nature can help you to be your most productive self, when you listen. Use the varying energy of the moon's cycles to your benefit. The demands of our modern world often make us feel that we need to be on top of our game every day. Being busy is almost treated as a badge of honour, but we are not supposed to be operating at one hundred percent every day of the month. We are cyclical beings. Rest and alone time also need to be honoured and included on our schedules with the same importance as any business meeting.

When we rest, we recharge and become our most productive selves. During the New Moon we set intentions for the month ahead, we are then free to move forward focussing on our goals, with a renewed clarity on what we want and heightened energy to get us there.

The aim of this diary is to help you organise busy schedules whilst avoiding burnout and feeling overwhelmed. When life flows easily, creativity and happiness will come to you in abundance.

Wishing you a very happy, productive year full of joy.

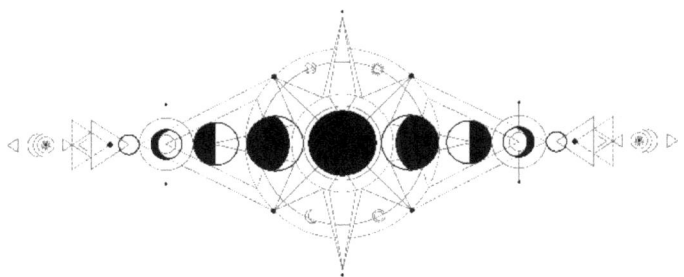

A **New Moon** is a monthly rebirth, a time for new beginnings, ideas and creativity. An opportunity to set your intentions. This is a perfect time to spend alone journaling your thoughts and practicing self care which will mean different things to all of you. Perhaps a morning meditation or an evening bubble bath is all it takes, but whatever it is, make sure to take some time for yourself. In the silence you will receive the intuitive guidance you need. Take some time to set your intentions for the month ahead.

Clear Quartz, a cleansing crystal perfect for clearing the mind and aiding in meditation.

The **Waxing Moon** asks you to act upon the ideas you received during the new moon. This is a perfect time for socialising and communication, so scheduling in meetings would be good during a waxing moon, but be careful not to burnout, eat well during this moon and avoid anything not so good for you.

Citrine, a wonderful crystal for manifesting abundance.

A **Full Moon** is a good time to check in with the intentions you set under the new moon. Consider what finishing touches you need to get you to your goals. Work with your intuition and gut feelings. Get clear on what you need to release when the moon begins to wane. Energies are very high under this powerful full moon phase, so you will have energy for meeting with friends, but you may prefer to use this energy to be at home burning your favourite incense, playing some music, and tuning into your highest self. Full moons are a great time to cleanse the body and mind.

Moonstone, helps to connect to your inner goddess and true meaning.

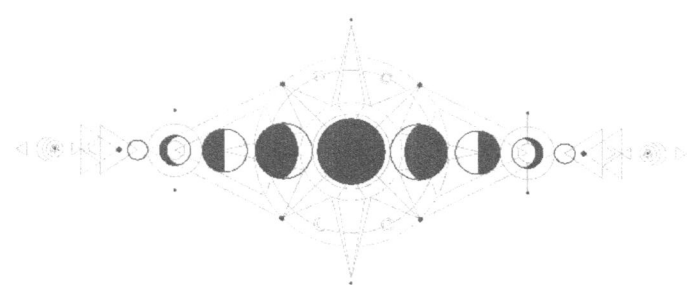

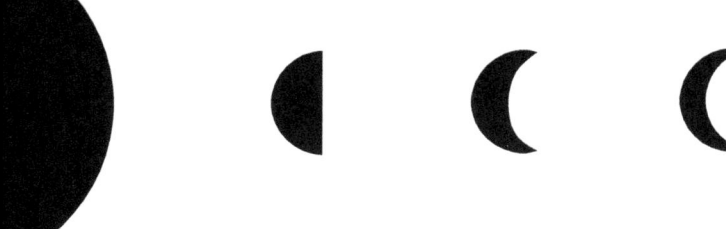

The **Waning Moon** calls you to release that which does not serve you. Pay attention to anything that has stood in the way of your goals and dreams. This is a perfect time to organise, throw things away, consider if you have any toxic elements in your life. Do you need to get rid of any particular bad habits? Now would be the time to start looking at that. Let go of unwanted energy and release.

Rhodonite, a healer related to the heart chakra which helps with forgiveness and releases self-destructive tendencies to help with healing at a soul level.

How amazing is the moon! She provides us with the chance to start afresh every month. We can use her energy to guide us. These points refer to how the moon affects us collectively, but each moon will affect us all slightly differently depending on our own birth charts. You may wish to dive deeper into this with an astrologer as it can be helpful for introspection and making sense of our experiences as we move throughout the year.

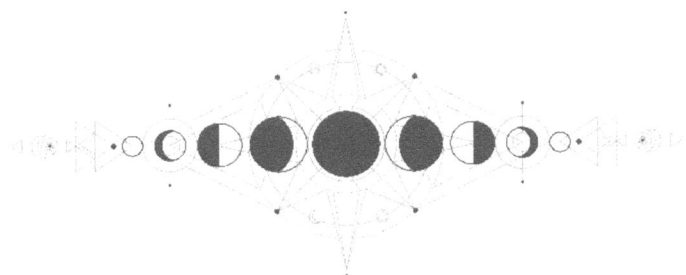

The Moon & The Zodiac

Aries - Birth and Manifestation
Fire Sign

Since Aries sits at the start of the astrological new year this **New Moon** (March) is the perfect time to start anew. A powerful portal for manifesting. Write down those intentions and go after whatever it is you feel passionate about.

An Aries **Full Moon** (October) has a way of bringing our fears and emotions to the surface. The ruling planet of Aries is Mars, there can be warrior energy and a competitive drive that surfaces. You may feel a call to action, but remember to release anything that no longer serves you.

Taurus - Grounded in Reality
Earth Sign

Being an earth sign the Taurus **New Moon** (April) helps us to feel grounded, and inspires us to cancel out the noise of other opinions so that we can hear what our own inner truth is. Taurus is ruled by Venus, she gives you permission to take care of yourself. If you need it go ahead and take time for yourself. Make sure your needs are being met.

The Taurus **Full Moon** (November) has a habit of bringing insecurities to the forefront, feelings around imposter syndrome and self worth may come up. It can be helpful to sit with these feelings, because we first need to acknowledge them in order to release them.

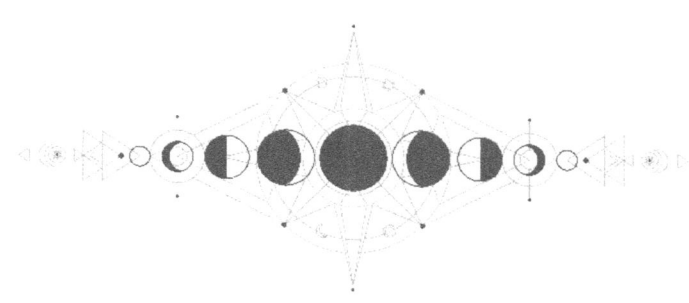

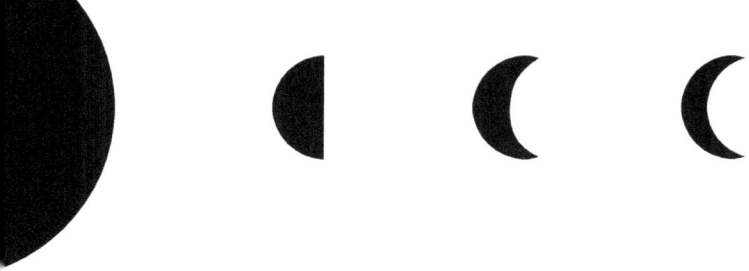

Gemini - Duality, Inspiration and Change
Air Sign

A Gemini **New Moon** (May) can often bring a feeling of excitement and inspiration. If however you are feeling drained and exhausted in the days leading up to this moon, it could be that you want to change something in your life but have been avoiding it. This moon will be eager to get your attention to encourage you to start taking action.

The Gemini **Full Moon** (December) can bring up a lot around communication and knowledge. Pay attention to what thoughts are coming up during this time. Lots of insights can come through, but thoughts may be in overdrive which can feel overwhelming and anxiety inducing. This is a good time to bring limiting beliefs to the surface, but remember to take time out and slow down, perhaps with yoga or breath work to stay centred.

Cancer - Sacred Depths of Intuition and Emotion
Water Sign

The Cancer **New Moon** (June) is very at home in her ruling planet of Cancer. This moon can bring up big emotions, a heightened sense of intuition and feminine power. Self care is important. Spend time alone or with people you can be vulnerable with. Wear your heart on your sleeve and really feel into everything that is stirring within you.

The Cancer **Full Moon** (January) may show you the road ahead. There can be a deep intensity that comes with this full moon. Cancer's intuitive energy helps to light the way. The sun is in Capricorn which brings ambition and visions for the future. Make the most of this combination to make plans for the year, create vision boards, get together with friends and plan summer adventures. Focus on anything that you need to change to get to where you want to be by this time next year.

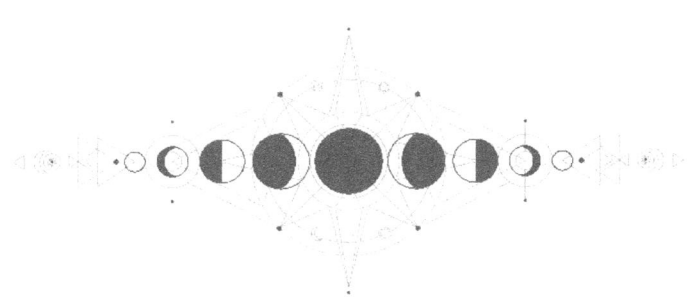

Leo - Charisma, Power and Heart-Centered Energy
Fire Sign

A **New Moon** in Leo (July) brings with it much power. The sun rules Leo, there is so much light, magnetism and energy. If you have been pondering over starting a new job, or adventure then this is the energy to use to get you there.

The **Full Moon** in Leo (February) has fiery energy which asks you to look at your desires beyond the to-do lists. What do you really want out of life? Where have you held yourself back to please others, where have you not lived your biggest dreams? Leo rules the heart and has a tendency to bring your desires to the surface. Spend some time in heart chakra meditation, really listen to what your heart is telling you. There's an element of bravery that comes with a Leo moon that will help you to put yourself first.

Virgo - Perfectionism and Attention to Detail
Earth Sign

Virgo is the healer so these **New Moon's** in Virgo (August&September!) offers deep healing for those willing to seek it. Yes, she is critical and we can expect to hear voices of self sabotage. Maybe we tell ourselves that our to do list is too big, we don't have time to sit and reflect during this moon, but if we give ourselves space and get honest, we can see big results. The ruling planet is Mercury which symbolises communication, travel and trade. Whilst Virgo energy brings organisation and focus. Use this combination, get a notepad, make some lists, do a clean out, cleanse your space and make room for your dreams.

The earthy energy of a **Full Moon** in Virgo (March) is so grounded that there is no where to hide from ourselves. This moon is a great time to check in with our lives in general, are we where we want to be? If not then we can use her creative, organisational energy to make a plan. What steps do you need to take to up-level your situation? Watch out for perfectionism and trying to control every outcome. Virgo brings great opportunity, but it is also nice to leave some things to the universe, she normally has something even better planned for us after all.

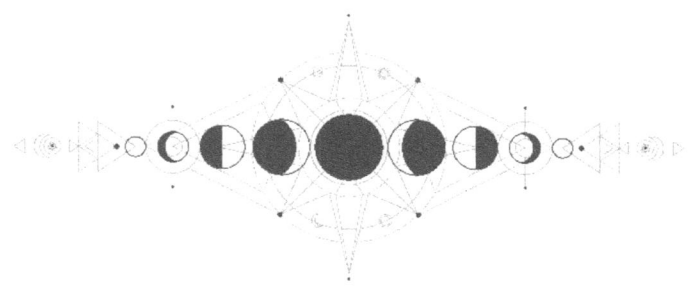

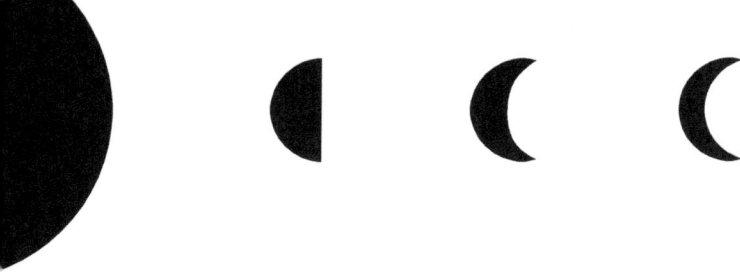

Libra - Balance and Relationships
Air Sign

The **New Moon** in Libra (October) brings up a lot around relationships, boundaries and balance. Use this moon to deepen the relationship you have with yourself. New moons are always a time for self reflection and inner work, but particularly around this Libra moon. Allow your intentions for the rest of the year and beyond to come through and watch out for any triggers that surface, especially around relationships or not speaking your truth.

Since the **Full Moon** in Libra (April) brings with it the energy of balance, it can be good practice to make a note of everything in your life that is important to you, make a circle and create 8 or 10 sections. Such as family life, romantic life, work life, health, fitness, travel, spiritual life etc. Then give a mark from one to ten. When you have finished you will have a picture of your life. It is likely that some areas score highly and others not so much. Where are you thriving? Which areas of your life/relationships do you need to work on?

Scorpio - Death and Rebirth
Water Sign

The **New Moon** in Scorpio (November) is an intense but brilliant moon that calls us to do the deepest shadow work. This often feels daunting. There is no where to run and hide under this moon. Emotions, deeply buried hurts and betrayals from our past can come up. Many people say they fear this moon and how it makes them feel, but really, there is much healing and change on the other side. Pluto the planet of death and destruction rules Scorpio, we can use this energy to make way for the new.

Under this **Full Moon** in Scorpio (May) spend some time in a sanctuary of your choice. Where do you feel safe? Perhaps in your favourite room at home with some incense burning whilst you relax under a duvet listening to music. Perhaps under your favourite tree. Where ever it is, try and carve out some time to yourself in a safe space. Once you are there close your eyes, take some breaths and think about what you need to release from your life. Perhaps it is clutter, a toxic relationship or working too many hours. What do you need to be free from, and how can you gently release yourself from it, so that you can be re-born, free from whatever was weighing you down.

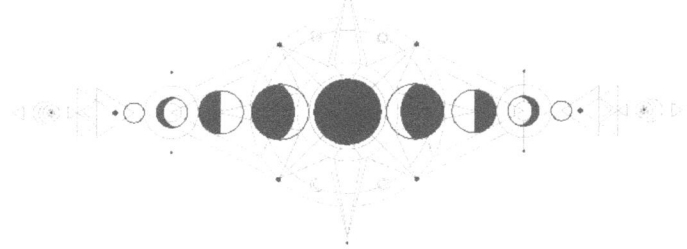

Sagittarius - Adventure, Freedom and Passion
Fire Sign

The **New Moon** in Sagittarius (December) brings freedom and adventure, but will highlight anywhere where you feel out of control. Are there systems of authority where you feel you lack autonomy? If so you could feel a bit suffocated by that under this moon. For the travellers and adventure seekers, this is the moon for you. We will be encouraged to get moving, take that trip, do all the big things we've been holding back from.

A **Full Moon** in Sagittarius (June) highlights anywhere where we might feel that we're being controlled, but the sun is in Gemini which brings the energy of change and truth, the ruling planet is Jupiter which symbolises abundance, fortune and expansion. The way forward will be illuminated. Spend some time alone, close out the noise and work out what you need to release, whilst getting clear on what you want to invite in.

Capricorn - Structure and Focus
Earth Sign

The **New Moon** in Capricorn is a very practical moon which doesn't really like anything too emotional. Get real under this energy about your life purpose and goals. Capricorn is ruled by Saturn which symbolises discipline and limitations. Set your inner practical self free to make plans for the year ahead, you may feel an element of productivity to finally get a certain project off the ground, and if you need to install some boundaries with others, that may well come to the surface (In 2025 we have two Virgo New Moons and no Capricorn New Moon)

Under this **Full Moon** in Capricorn (July) you may feel a need to organise the spaces around you: your home, office, wardrobe. Removing anything that is in your way.

Whilst Capricorn is practical, the sun is in Cancer which brings the deeper emotions to the surface, and sometimes this can manifest as doubt. You may doubt your ability to start your own business or travel round the world solo, these doubts are highlighting fears that have been hidden bring them to the surface and try and find the root cause for these limiting beliefs. Allow yourself to embrace these dreams. from a fresh perspective.

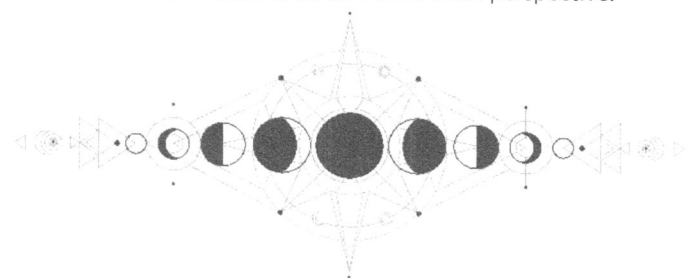

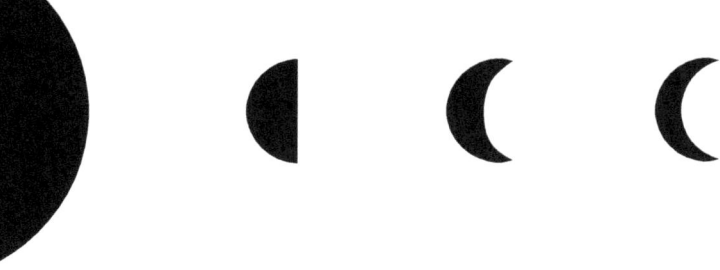

Aquarius - Innovation and Self Expression
Air Sign

The **New Moon** in Aquarius (January) brings visionary transmissions, and big picture views into the future. There's a fiercely independent energy that comes with this moon, so you may find yourself longing for freedom in any areas where that may be threatened. A tendency to rebel often emerges if this is the case.
You may feel a strong pull to be of service to others or mother earth in some way.
This moon is a good time to think about your passions, what would you love to spend every day doing? If that's not already your life, what steps can you take to get there?

The **Full Moon** in Aquarius (August) is a moon that brings with it the potential for change. The freedom loving energy of Aquarius with the sun in Leo brings a chance to connect to heart centred Leo energy as well, this combination is perfect. Tune in to listen to your hearts desires, whilst using innovative Aquarius to visualise how you can make this a reality in the coming months.

Pisces - Mystical and Dreamy
Water Sign

The **New Moon** in Pisces (February) brings mystical, dreamy energy. The last sign of the zodiac helps you to see into the beyond. The Pisces symbol is two fish swimming in opposite directions, a nod to the hermetic principle 'as above so below'.

Daydream to your hearts content under this whimsical moon, journal about the visions that come through to you. Create vision boards, fill out the manifestation pages in this diary or any other manifestation techniques you like to use. This is a great moon for it.

The last **Full Moon** of the summer (September) before moving into autumn is a good time for reflection. Check in with yourself, what has shifted for you since the summer solstice? Have you dealt with any challenges, if so have you learned lessons that have helped you to grow? The sun is in Virgo so there is an opportunity to harness the practical energy of Virgo alongside dreamy visionary Pisces. This is a really powerful combination to work with. Release anything your holding on to so that you can move forwards with the visions that come through from Pisces.

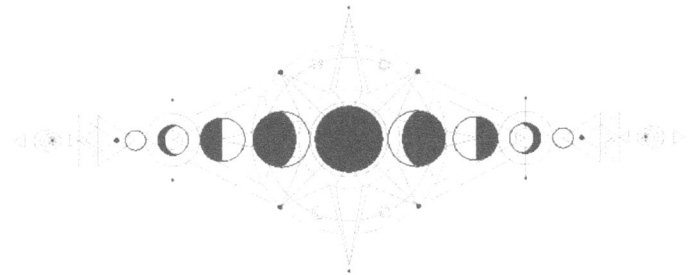

The Blood Mysteries and the Moon

'Your Moon Time'

Follicular - Inner Spring - Maiden - Waxing Moon

Ovulation - Inner Summer - Mother - Full Moon

Luteal - Inner Autumn - Sorceress - Waning Moon

Menstruation - Inner Winter - Crone - New Moon

The White Moon Cycle
Bleed with the new moon - Ovulate with the full moon
Mirroring the moons cycle
Embodying creation whether that be children or ideas and projects that are being brought to life.

The Red Moon Cycle
Bleed with the full moon - Ovulate with the new moon
Embodying the medicine woman. In ancient times this cycle was for the priestess and healers who channelled their energy outwards.

The Pink Moon Cycle
Bleed with the waxing crescent - Ovulate with the waning crescent.
Embodying expansion and spiritual ascension, becoming a new version of yourself.

The Purple Moon Cycle
Bleed with the waning crescent - Ovulate with the waxing crescent
Embodying release and desire for inner reflection.

It is said that during ancient times when we lived in hunter gatherer communities we would all have been in sync experiencing a white moon cycle together, with the exception of the priestess who would have been on the red moon cycle.

Back when there was no light pollution we lived in tune with our circadian rhythms, the outer seasonal cycles and our own inner hormonal cycles. We lived as cyclical beings and women gathered in circle together during their moon time, holding space for each other and shedding all that no longer served them. They would sit in ceremony, their cycle was a spiritual practice.

Today it is recognised that our periods are our fifth vital sign. We know they can tell us a great deal about our health in general. Our energy waxes and wanes through-out the month just like the moon does.

It is good practice to chart our cycles, and this includes those of us who don't have a menstrual cycle. It can still be very beneficial to chart our states of being on a daily basis allowing us to notice any patterns over the period of a few months. This is a useful tool in getting to know subtleties about yourself. You can then use this information to work in harmony with your inner ebbs and flows. For example if you see that you are always exhausted on day twenty, but full of life on day twelve then you can use this information to your advantage.

There is space in this diary to make notes each day. Start on day one of your cycle and write a note on each day about anything you feel you would like to chart, particularly your emotions and energy levels. Try it out and see if you notice a pattern. If you do not have a cycle, perhaps use the new moon as your day one.

Honouring the seasons

Paying close attention to the seasons and creating rituals around them helps us in turn to honour ourselves. We are nature. We are cyclical beings. When we move with the natural rhythms of our Earth, we learn to live in a flow state, in the present. As each season moves into the next on the wheel of the year, we can celebrate these changes outside and inside of ourselves. Equinoxes and solstices allow us to feel at one with the seasons and remind us to check in with ourselves, so rather than mindlessly racing through the year wondering how another one flew by so quickly, working with the seasons can add focus and clarity to these 365 days.

Spring Equinox 20th March

A time when light and dark come into balance and nature blooms with life. Use this time to think about what seeds you want to sow in your own life. How do you want to use this new vital energy to manifest abundance? Spring shows us how to be patient whilst we wait for the little buds to blossom. Emulate nature in this way and be easy on yourself if you are waiting for your manifestations to come to fruition. Try and spend at least ten minutes every day with your bare feet touching the Earth. Take as much time in nature as you can, pausing to pay attention to spring as she emerges from the dark winter. Close your eyes and take in the sounds of nature all around you. Spend time journaling on your goals for the remainder of the year. Are there steps you can now take as you leave winter behind you to get ready to step into the light of spring?

Ritual ideas: Cleanse your space with frankincense or incense of your choice, do a grounding meditation such as a root chakra meditation by imagining that your feet root firmly into the Earth, you could sit with your back against a tree for twenty minutes connecting with the Earth's energy, followed by a cleansing bath with Epsom salts and rose petals.

Summer Solstice 21st June

In the northern hemisphere the Earth's axis is tilted at its closest point from the sun. This is the longest day, and shortest night. Nature is in full bloom all around us and inspires us to put our creative ideas into practice and bring projects to life. Use the heightened energy of the solstice to create and be inspired.

Ritual Ideas: Get outside, walk barefoot through a forest, hold a fire circle with friends. Celebrate nature and each other. Eat fresh food from the Earth and give thanks for all that she provides us. Write lists of everything you are grateful for. What is showing up in abundance for you? Stop and pause to give thanks for it. Get up at sunrise to honour the sun. Perhaps incorporate a yoga session or whatever suits you to move your body. Get creative with your celebrations and make them your own.

Autumn Equinox 22nd September
The first day of autumn is a time for releasing. Get clear on what no longer serves you, and just like the trees who shed their leaves, allow yourself to let go. The days will begin to get shorter and nature invites you to retreat inwards to rejuvenate. There is a different level of energy that we are now heading into, and one of the best ways to honour that time is to reflect on the year so far, and ask what you need to shed to move forward.

Ritual ideas: Write a list of anything you don't want to take with you as we move into this next part of the year, make a bonfire and burn the list. Take a long walk and notice the changes in nature all around you and take home some moss and wood to make an altar for the Earth goddess Gaia. As the nights get shorter and the air gets colder embrace the change in energy and the subtle whispers calling you inwards.

Winter Solstice 21st December
Celebrate the cyclical nature of our world on the longest night before the sun is renewed once more. The winter solstice welcomes a slower pace, honour that. Reclaim the stillness. The darkness of winter can be difficult, try and notice the beauty of the sparse trees and frosty mornings. Treat yourself to comforting foods and special time with loved ones playing board games and embrace the slower, quieter, darker days.

Ritual ideas: Spend some time in silence reflecting on the year so far and your dreams for the year ahead. Head to a beauty spot that you have a connection with and reflect on any changes to this area during winter. Wrap up warm and enjoy a fire, the flames can be very meditative and healing. Shamans say that fire allows for rapid transformation. Make the most of the darkness and any revelations it has helped bring to light.

Wheel of the Year

* Yule - December 21st
Yule is the winter festival celebrating the winter solstice and the returning of the light.

* Imbolc - February 1st - Sunset on February 2nd
This festival marks the beginning of spring. Goddess Bridgid is celebrated with feasts and fires. Green candles are lit in her honour.

* Ostara - March 20th
A solar holiday where we welcome the returning warmth of spring. Goddess Eostre is honoured with alters of flowers, eggs and seeds.

* Beltane - May 1st
The half way mark between the spring equinox and summer solstice. We give thanks to the fertility of the land.

* Litha - June 20th
The longest day of the year. Vikings would pray to Freyja for an abundant harvest and ceremonial plants are used around midsummer bonfires.

* Lammas - August 1st
Represents the midway point between summer and autumn. The time of the first harvest.

* Mabon - September 22nd
The second harvest which lands on the autumn equinox.

* Samhian - October 31st
Better known as halloween this is the Celtic new year and the final harvest. The veil between worlds is at its thinnest, we honour our ancestors on this night.

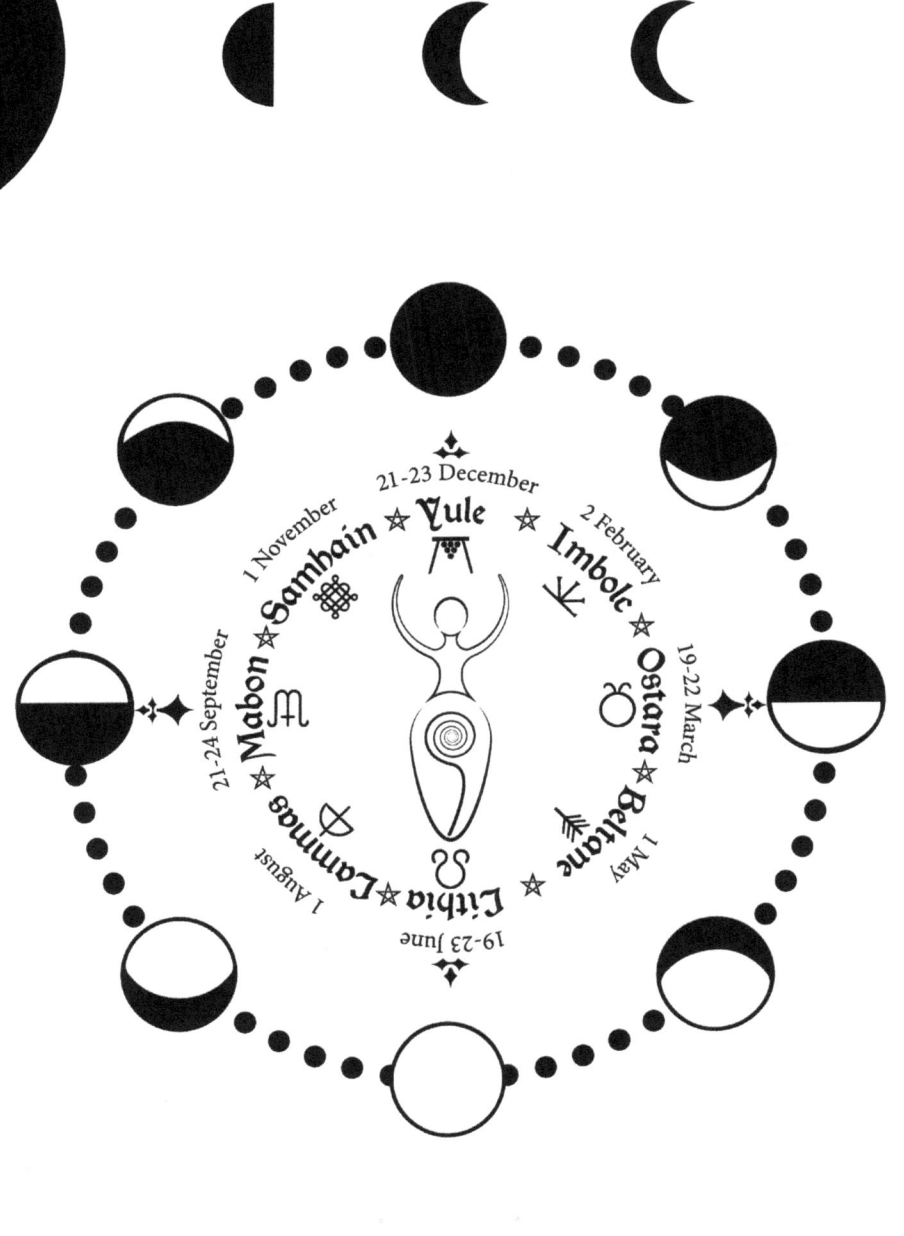

Three ways to manifest your dreams

New Years resolutions are a cultural norm for many of us, but often we find it difficult to commit. It may be that the depth of winter just isn't the right time for making big decisions for the next twelve months. Some of us prefer to write down our visions for the year around the spring equinox when the world around us is coming to life.

There is no right or wrong. Fill in the goals pages at whatever time of year feels right to you.

There are many ways to bring our creative visions to life, and you will find more than one way to manifest your dreams in this diary. Yearly goal setting, seasonal visions plus a vision board.

On the opposite page you can write out your main yearly goal, with space to break it down. Work out what you need to do daily, weekly and monthly to get you to where you want to be by 2026.

There is also space for seasonal inspiration. Spend some time each equinox and solstice quietly observing and making space for inspiration to come through. Take some time out with a warm drink, a candle and something that represents the season, perhaps a flower, certain colours or a crystal, and allow yourself to visualise your desires for the season ahead. As mother Earth moves through her cycles we often find that ideas come to us that we never would have thought of during the darker days around New Year. Manifesting alongside the seasons adds a beautiful dimension to making our dreams a reality.

My main yearly goal is: _____

To achieve this goal by 2026, I will create the following habits to get myself there.

Daily

Weekly

Monthly

Seasonal Vision for 2025

Use this space to write any ideas that come to you throughout the year. From Inspirational business ideas, passion projects or perhaps countries you want to visit.

Winter

Spring

Summer

Autumn

Vision board

Use this space to paint, doodle or cut pictures out of magazines. Whatever works for you. The goal is to create a powerful visualisation tool to aid in manifesting your dreams. You can look at this every day to bring your 2025 goals to life.

Share your vision with us on Instagram @the_moonmethod

"Practice listening to your intuition, your inner voice; ask questions; be curious; see what you see; hear what you hear; and then act upon what you know to be true. These intuitive powers were given to your soul at birth."

—Clarissa Pinkola Estés.

Listen to your intuition

Make notes here when you notice that you have listened to or ignored your inner compass. The more we pay attention the more attuned we become...

January 2025

Notes	Monday	Tuesday	Wednesday
	30	31	1
	6	7	8
	13	14	15
	20	21	22
	27	28	29

Thursday	Friday	Saturday	Sunday
2	3	4	5
9	10	11	12
16	17	18	19
23	24	25	26
30	31		

January
Goddess Minerva

MINERVA

Roman Goddess of wisdom, the arts and strategy in war.
She was skilled in healing, medicine, poetry and crafts.
It is said that she invented the flute. No wonder Ovid called her
'the goddess of a thousand works.'

Along with Jupiter and Juno she was worshipped on Capitoline Hill as a patron of the city.

She had many temples and festivals dedicated to her throughout Rome, even today her statues can still be found in institutions throughout the city.

Standing the test of time as a symbol of wisdom.

Book: Queendom by Malka Russell
Song: Medicine by Rising Appalachia
Moon Phase: Waxing
Crystal: Amethyst

My Vision for January

Wednesday | 1 January 2025 - Waxing Cresecent

6:00		Today's quick wins	
7:00			
8:00			
9:00			
10:00			
11:00		Health and nutrition	
12:00			
13:00			
14:00		Today, I am grateful for…	
15:00			
16:00			
17:00		Today's self care	
18:00			
19:00			
20:00		Chart your cycle	
21:00			
22:00			
23:00		Positive affirmation	
Notes			

Thursday | 2 January 2025 - Waxing Cresecent

6:00	**Today's quick wins**
7:00	
8:00	
9:00	
10:00	
11:00	**Health and nutrition**
12:00	
13:00	
14:00	**Today, I am grateful for...**
15:00	
16:00	
17:00	**Today's self care**
18:00	
19:00	
20:00	**Chart your cycle**
21:00	
22:00	
23:00	**Positive affirmation**
Notes	

Friday | 3 January 2025 - Waxing Cresecent

6:00	Today's quick wins	
7:00		
8:00		
9:00		
10:00		
11:00	Health and nutrition	
12:00		
13:00		
14:00	Today, I am grateful for…	
15:00		
16:00		
17:00	Today's self care	
18:00		
19:00		
20:00	Chart your cycle	
21:00		
22:00		
23:00	Positive affirmation	
Notes		

Saturday | 4 January 2025 - Waxing Cresecent

6:00	Today's quick wins
7:00	
8:00	
9:00	
10:00	
11:00	Health and nutrition
12:00	
13:00	
14:00	Today, I am grateful for...
15:00	
16:00	
17:00	Today's self care
18:00	
19:00	
20:00	Chart your cycle
21:00	
22:00	
23:00	Positive affirmation
Notes	

Sunday | 5 January 2025 - Waxing Cresecent

6:00		Today's quick wins
7:00		
8:00		
9:00		
10:00		
11:00		Health and nutrition
12:00		
13:00		
14:00		Today, I am grateful for…
15:00		
16:00		
17:00		Today's self care
18:00		
19:00		
20:00		Chart your cycle
21:00		
22:00		
23:00		Positive affirmation
Notes		

Monday | 6 January 2025 - First Quarter

6:00	Today's quick wins
7:00	
8:00	
9:00	
10:00	
11:00	Health and nutrition
12:00	
13:00	
14:00	Today, I am grateful for...
15:00	
16:00	
17:00	Today's self care
18:00	
19:00	
20:00	Chart your cycle
21:00	
22:00	
23:00	Positive affirmation
Notes	

Tuesday | 7 January 2025 - First Quarter

6:00		Today's quick wins
7:00		
8:00		
9:00		
10:00		
11:00		Health and nutrition
12:00		
13:00		
14:00		Today, I am grateful for...
15:00		
16:00		
17:00		Today's self care
18:00		
19:00		
20:00		Chart your cycle
21:00		
22:00		
23:00		Positive affirmation
Notes		

Wednesday | 8 January 2025 - Waxing Gibbous

6:00	Today's quick wins
7:00	
8:00	
9:00	
10:00	
11:00	Health and nutrition
12:00	
13:00	
14:00	Today, I am grateful for…
15:00	
16:00	
17:00	Today's self care
18:00	
19:00	
20:00	Chart your cycle
21:00	
22:00	
23:00	Positive affirmation
Notes	

Thursday | 9 January 2025 - Waxing Gibbous

6:00		Today's quick wins	
7:00			
8:00			
9:00			
10:00			
11:00		Health and nutrition	
12:00			
13:00			
14:00		Today, I am grateful for…	
15:00			
16:00			
17:00		Today's self care	
18:00			
19:00			
20:00		Chart your cycle	
21:00			
22:00			
23:00		Positive affirmation	
Notes			

Friday | 10 January 2025 - Waxing Gibbous

6:00		Today's quick wins	
7:00			
8:00			
9:00			
10:00			
11:00		Health and nutrition	
12:00			
13:00			
14:00		Today, I am grateful for...	
15:00			
16:00			
17:00		Today's self care	
18:00			
19:00			
20:00		Chart your cycle	
21:00			
22:00			
23:00		Positive affirmation	
Notes			

Saturday | 11 January 2025 - Waxing Gibbous

6:00	Today's quick wins	
7:00		
8:00		
9:00		
10:00		
11:00	Health and nutrition	
12:00		
13:00		
14:00	Today, I am grateful for…	
15:00		
16:00		
17:00	Today's self care	
18:00		
19:00		
20:00	Chart your cycle	
21:00		
22:00		
23:00	Positive affirmation	
Notes		

Sunday | 12 January 2025 - Waxing Gibbous

6:00	Today's quick wins
7:00	
8:00	
9:00	
10:00	
11:00	Health and nutrition
12:00	
13:00	
14:00	Today, I am grateful for...
15:00	
16:00	
17:00	Today's self care
18:00	
19:00	
20:00	Chart your cycle
21:00	
22:00	
23:00	Positive affirmation
Notes	

Monday | 13 January 2025 - Full Moon in Cancer at 22.26 GMT

6:00	Today's quick wins	
7:00		
8:00		
9:00		
10:00		
11:00	Health and nutrition	
12:00		
13:00		
14:00	Today, I am grateful for…	
15:00		
16:00		
17:00	Today's self care	
18:00		
19:00		
20:00	Chart your cycle	
21:00		
22:00		
23:00	Positive affirmation	
Notes		

Tuesday | 14 January 2025 - Waning Gibbous

6:00	**Today's quick wins**
7:00	
8:00	
9:00	
10:00	
11:00	**Health and nutrition**
12:00	
13:00	
14:00	**Today, I am grateful for...**
15:00	
16:00	
17:00	**Today's self care**
18:00	
19:00	
20:00	**Chart your cycle**
21:00	
22:00	
23:00	**Positive affirmation**
Notes	

Wednesday | 15 January 2025 - Waning Gibbous

6:00		Today's quick wins
7:00		
8:00		
9:00		
10:00		
11:00		Health and nutrition
12:00		
13:00		
14:00		Today, I am grateful for...
15:00		
16:00		
17:00		Today's self care
18:00		
19:00		
20:00		Chart your cycle
21:00		
22:00		
23:00		Positive affirmation
Notes		

Thursday | 16 January 2025 - Waning Gibbous

6:00	**Today's quick wins**
7:00	
8:00	
9:00	
10:00	
11:00	**Health and nutrition**
12:00	
13:00	
14:00	**Today, I am grateful for…**
15:00	
16:00	
17:00	**Today's self care**
18:00	
19:00	
20:00	**Chart your cycle**
21:00	
22:00	
23:00	**Positive affirmation**
Notes	

Friday | 17 January 2025 - Waning Gibbous

6:00	Today's quick wins
7:00	
8:00	
9:00	
10:00	
11:00	Health and nutrition
12:00	
13:00	
14:00	Today, I am grateful for...
15:00	
16:00	
17:00	Today's self care
18:00	
19:00	
20:00	Chart your cycle
21:00	
22:00	
23:00	Positive affirmation
Notes	

Saturday | 18 January 2025 - Waning Gibbous

6:00	**Today's quick wins**
7:00	
8:00	
9:00	
10:00	
11:00	**Health and nutrition**
12:00	
13:00	
14:00	**Today, I am grateful for...**
15:00	
16:00	
17:00	**Today's self care**
18:00	
19:00	
20:00	**Chart your cycle**
21:00	
22:00	
23:00	**Positive affirmation**
Notes	

Sunday | 19 January 2025 - Waning Gibbous

6:00	Today's quick wins	
7:00		
8:00		
9:00		
10:00		
11:00	Health and nutrition	
12:00		
13:00		
14:00	Today, I am grateful for...	
15:00		
16:00		
17:00	Today's self care	
18:00		
19:00		
20:00	Chart your cycle	
21:00		
22:00		
23:00	Positive affirmation	
Notes		

Monday | 20 January 2025 - Waning Gibbous

6:00	Today's quick wins
7:00	
8:00	
9:00	
10:00	
11:00	Health and nutrition
12:00	
13:00	
14:00	Today, I am grateful for…
15:00	
16:00	
17:00	Today's self care
18:00	
19:00	
20:00	Chart your cycle
21:00	
22:00	
23:00	Positive affirmation
Notes	

Tuesday | 21 January 2025 - Last Quarter

6:00	**Today's quick wins**
7:00	
8:00	
9:00	
10:00	
11:00	**Health and nutrition**
12:00	
13:00	
14:00	**Today, I am grateful for...**
15:00	
16:00	
17:00	**Today's self care**
18:00	
19:00	
20:00	**Chart your cycle**
21:00	
22:00	
23:00	**Positive affirmation**
Notes	

Wednesday | 22 January 2025 - Last Quarter

6:00		Today's quick wins	
7:00			
8:00			
9:00			
10:00			
11:00		Health and nutrition	
12:00			
13:00			
14:00		Today, I am grateful for...	
15:00			
16:00			
17:00		Today's self care	
18:00			
19:00			
20:00		Chart your cycle	
21:00			
22:00			
23:00		Positive affirmation	
Notes			

Thursday | 23 January 2025 - Waning Crescent

6:00		Today's quick wins	
7:00			
8:00			
9:00			
10:00			
11:00		Health and nutrition	
12:00			
13:00			
14:00		Today, I am grateful for...	
15:00			
16:00			
17:00		Today's self care	
18:00			
19:00			
20:00		Chart your cycle	
21:00			
22:00			
23:00		Positive affirmation	
Notes			

Friday | 24 January 2025 - Waning Crescent

6:00		Today's quick wins	
7:00			
8:00			
9:00			
10:00			
11:00		Health and nutrition	
12:00			
13:00			
14:00		Today, I am grateful for…	
15:00			
16:00			
17:00		Today's self care	
18:00			
19:00			
20:00		Chart your cycle	
21:00			
22:00			
23:00		Positive affirmation	
Notes			

Saturday | 25 January 2025 - Waning Crescent

6:00	Today's quick wins	
7:00		
8:00		
9:00		
10:00		
11:00	Health and nutrition	
12:00		
13:00		
14:00	Today, I am grateful for…	
15:00		
16:00		
17:00	Today's self care	
18:00		
19:00		
20:00	Chart your cycle	
21:00		
22:00		
23:00	Positive affirmation	
Notes		

Sunday | 26 January 2025 - Waning Crescent

6:00	Today's quick wins	
7:00		
8:00		
9:00		
10:00		
11:00	Health and nutrition	
12:00		
13:00		
14:00	Today, I am grateful for...	
15:00		
16:00		
17:00	Today's self care	
18:00		
19:00		
20:00	Chart your cycle	
21:00		
22:00		
23:00	Positive affirmation	
Notes		

Monday | 27 January 2025 - Waning Crescent

6:00	**Today's quick wins**
7:00	
8:00	
9:00	
10:00	
11:00	**Health and nutrition**
12:00	
13:00	
14:00	**Today, I am grateful for...**
15:00	
16:00	
17:00	**Today's self care**
18:00	
19:00	
20:00	**Chart your cycle**
21:00	
22:00	
23:00	**Positive affirmation**
Notes	

Tuesday | 28 January 2025 - Waning Crescent

6:00		Today's quick wins	
7:00			
8:00			
9:00			
10:00			
11:00		Health and nutrition	
12:00			
13:00			
14:00		Today, I am grateful for…	
15:00			
16:00			
17:00		Today's self care	
18:00			
19:00			
20:00		Chart your cycle	
21:00			
22:00			
23:00		Positive affirmation	
Notes			

Wednesday | 29 January 2025 - New Moon in Aquarius at 12.35 GMT

6:00	**Today's quick wins**
7:00	
8:00	
9:00	
10:00	
11:00	**Health and nutrition**
12:00	
13:00	
14:00	**Today, I am grateful for...**
15:00	
16:00	
17:00	**Today's self care**
18:00	
19:00	
20:00	**Chart your cycle**
21:00	
22:00	
23:00	**Positive affirmation**
Notes	

Thursday | 30 January 2025 - Waxing Crescent

6:00	Today's quick wins	
7:00		
8:00		
9:00		
10:00		
11:00	Health and nutrition	
12:00		
13:00		
14:00	Today, I am grateful for...	
15:00		
16:00		
17:00	Today's self care	
18:00		
19:00		
20:00	Chart your cycle	
21:00		
22:00		
23:00	Positive affirmation	
Notes		

Friday | 31 January 2025 - Waxing Crescent

6:00		Today's quick wins	
7:00			
8:00			
9:00			
10:00			
11:00		Health and nutrition	
12:00			
13:00			
14:00		Today, I am grateful for…	
15:00			
16:00			
17:00		Today's self care	
18:00			
19:00			
20:00		Chart your cycle	
21:00			
22:00			
23:00		Positive affirmation	
Notes			

January achievements

Be proud of yourself and all that you have achieved this month. Write down your wins, big and small. If you have not achieved everything that you set out to do, that's okay! We learn and grow through our mistakes and experiences. You can use this space to make notes about anything that you have learned.

February 2025

Notes	Monday	Tuesday	Wednesday
	27	28	29
	3	4	5
	10	11	12
	17	18	19
	24	25	26

Thursday	Friday	Saturday	Sunday
30	31	1	3
6	7	8	9
13	14	15	16
20 ☾	21	22	23
27	28 ●	1	2

February
Goddess Nut

NUT

Goddess of the Sky and Heavens.

Nut is often depicted as a woman bent over the earth with her head in the West and feet in the East.

She protects the dead until they pass over into the next life.

Ancient myths tell us that Nut eats the sun god Ra every night and gives birth to him every morning.

Festivals were held for her in late February.

Book: The Goddess Nut: And the Wisdom of the Sky by Lesley Jackson and Brian Andrews
Song: On the Transit of Venus by Phil Thornton
Moon phase: Dark moon
Crystal: Lapis Lazuli

My Vision for February

Go confidently in the direction of your dreams! Live the life you've imagined. As you simplify your life, the laws of the universe will be simpler – Henry David Thoreau

In what ways can you simplify your life?
Are you holding on to clothes you have not worn in years, or perhaps your to do list is so long it is impossible to achieve. Make some notes on what actions you can take to simplify your life and space.

Saturday | 1 February 2025 - Waxing Crescent

6:00	**Today's quick wins**
7:00	
8:00	
9:00	
10:00	
11:00	**Health and nutrition**
12:00	
13:00	
14:00	**Today, I am grateful for...**
15:00	
16:00	
17:00	**Today's self care**
18:00	
19:00	
20:00	**Chart your cycle**
21:00	
22:00	
23:00	**Positive affirmation**
Notes	

Sunday | 2 February 2025 - Waxing Crescent

6:00		Today's quick wins
7:00		
8:00		
9:00		
10:00		
11:00		Health and nutrition
12:00		
13:00		
14:00		Today, I am grateful for...
15:00		
16:00		
17:00		Today's self care
18:00		
19:00		
20:00		Chart your cycle
21:00		
22:00		
23:00		Positive affirmation
Notes		

Monday | 3 February 2025 - Waxing Crescent

6:00	Today's quick wins	
7:00		
8:00		
9:00		
10:00		
11:00	Health and nutrition	
12:00		
13:00		
14:00	Today, I am grateful for…	
15:00		
16:00		
17:00	Today's self care	
18:00		
19:00		
20:00	Chart your cycle	
21:00		
22:00		
23:00	Positive affirmation	
Notes		

Tuesday | 4 February 2025 - Waxing Crescent

6:00	**Today's quick wins**
7:00	
8:00	
9:00	
10:00	
11:00	**Health and nutrition**
12:00	
13:00	
14:00	**Today, I am grateful for...**
15:00	
16:00	
17:00	**Today's self care**
18:00	
19:00	
20:00	**Chart your cycle**
21:00	
22:00	
23:00	**Positive affirmation**
Notes	

Wednesday | 5 February 2025 - First Quarter

6:00	Today's quick wins	
7:00		
8:00		
9:00		
10:00		
11:00	Health and nutrition	
12:00		
13:00		
14:00	Today, I am grateful for…	
15:00		
16:00		
17:00	Today's self care	
18:00		
19:00		
20:00	Chart your cycle	
21:00		
22:00		
23:00	Positive affirmation	
Notes		

Thursday | 6 February 2025 - Waxing Gibbous

6:00	Today's quick wins
7:00	
8:00	
9:00	
10:00	
11:00	Health and nutrition
12:00	
13:00	
14:00	Today, I am grateful for...
15:00	
16:00	
17:00	Today's self care
18:00	
19:00	
20:00	Chart your cycle
21:00	
22:00	
23:00	Positive affirmation
Notes	

Friday | 7 February 2025 - Waxing Gibbous

6:00	Today's quick wins	
7:00		
8:00		
9:00		
10:00		
11:00	Health and nutrition	
12:00		
13:00		
14:00	Today, I am grateful for...	
15:00		
16:00		
17:00	Today's self care	
18:00		
19:00		
20:00	Chart your cycle	
21:00		
22:00		
23:00	Positive affirmation	
Notes		

Saturday | 8 February 2025 - Waxing Gibbous

6:00	**Today's quick wins**
7:00	
8:00	
9:00	
10:00	
11:00	**Health and nutrition**
12:00	
13:00	
14:00	**Today, I am grateful for…**
15:00	
16:00	
17:00	**Today's self care**
18:00	
19:00	
20:00	**Chart your cycle**
21:00	
22:00	
23:00	**Positive affirmation**
Notes	

Sunday | 9 February 2025 - Waxing Gibbous

6:00	Today's quick wins	
7:00		
8:00		
9:00		
10:00		
11:00	Health and nutrition	
12:00		
13:00		
14:00	Today, I am grateful for...	
15:00		
16:00		
17:00	Today's self care	
18:00		
19:00		
20:00	Chart your cycle	
21:00		
22:00		
23:00	Positive affirmation	
Notes		

Monday | 10 February 2025 - Waxing Gibbous

6:00		Today's quick wins
7:00		
8:00		
9:00		
10:00		
11:00		Health and nutrition
12:00		
13:00		
14:00		Today, I am grateful for...
15:00		
16:00		
17:00		Today's self care
18:00		
19:00		
20:00		Chart your cycle
21:00		
22:00		
23:00		Positive affirmation
Notes		

Tuesday | 11 February 2025 - Waxing Gibbous

6:00	Today's quick wins	
7:00		
8:00		
9:00		
10:00		
11:00	Health and nutrition	
12:00		
13:00		
14:00	Today, I am grateful for...	
15:00		
16:00		
17:00	Today's self care	
18:00		
19:00		
20:00	Chart your cycle	
21:00		
22:00		
23:00	Positive affirmation	
Notes		

Wednesday | 12 February 2025 - Full Moon In Leo 13.53 GMT

6:00		Today's quick wins
7:00		
8:00		
9:00		
10:00		
11:00		Health and nutrition
12:00		
13:00		
14:00		Today, I am grateful for…
15:00		
16:00		
17:00		Today's self care
18:00		
19:00		
20:00		Chart your cycle
21:00		
22:00		
23:00		Positive affirmation
Notes		

Thursday | 13 February 2025 - Waning Gibbous

6:00	Today's quick wins
7:00	
8:00	
9:00	
10:00	
11:00	Health and nutrition
12:00	
13:00	
14:00	Today, I am grateful for...
15:00	
16:00	
17:00	Today's self care
18:00	
19:00	
20:00	Chart your cycle
21:00	
22:00	
23:00	Positive affirmation
Notes	

Friday | 14 February 2025 - Waning Gibbous

6:00		Today's quick wins
7:00		
8:00		
9:00		
10:00		
11:00		Health and nutrition
12:00		
13:00		
14:00		Today, I am grateful for...
15:00		
16:00		
17:00		Today's self care
18:00		
19:00		
20:00		Chart your cycle
21:00		
22:00		
23:00		Positive affirmation
Notes		

Saturday | 15 February 2025 - Waning Gibbous

6:00	**Today's quick wins**
7:00	
8:00	
9:00	
10:00	
11:00	**Health and nutrition**
12:00	
13:00	
14:00	**Today, I am grateful for...**
15:00	
16:00	
17:00	**Today's self care**
18:00	
19:00	
20:00	**Chart your cycle**
21:00	
22:00	
23:00	**Positive affirmation**
Notes	

Sunday | 16 February 2025 - Waning Gibbous

6:00	**Today's quick wins**
7:00	
8:00	
9:00	
10:00	
11:00	**Health and nutrition**
12:00	
13:00	
14:00	**Today, I am grateful for...**
15:00	
16:00	
17:00	**Today's self care**
18:00	
19:00	
20:00	**Chart your cycle**
21:00	
22:00	
23:00	**Positive affirmation**
Notes	

Monday | 17 February 2025 - Waning Gibbous

6:00	Today's quick wins	
7:00		
8:00		
9:00		
10:00		
11:00	Health and nutrition	
12:00		
13:00		
14:00	Today, I am grateful for...	
15:00		
16:00		
17:00	Today's self care	
18:00		
19:00		
20:00	Chart your cycle	
21:00		
22:00		
23:00	Positive affirmation	
Notes		

Tuesday | 18 February 2025 - Waning Gibbous

6:00		Today's quick wins	
7:00			
8:00			
9:00			
10:00			
11:00		Health and nutrition	
12:00			
13:00			
14:00		Today, I am grateful for…	
15:00			
16:00			
17:00		Today's self care	
18:00			
19:00			
20:00		Chart your cycle	
21:00			
22:00			
23:00		Positive affirmation	
Notes			

Wednesday | 19 February 2025 - Waning Gibbous

6:00	**Today's quick wins**
7:00	
8:00	
9:00	
10:00	
11:00	**Health and nutrition**
12:00	
13:00	
14:00	**Today, I am grateful for…**
15:00	
16:00	
17:00	**Today's self care**
18:00	
19:00	
20:00	**Chart your cycle**
21:00	
22:00	
23:00	**Positive affirmation**
Notes	

Thursday | 20 February 2025 - Last Quarter

6:00	**Today's quick wins**
7:00	
8:00	
9:00	
10:00	
11:00	**Health and nutrition**
12:00	
13:00	
14:00	**Today, I am grateful for…**
15:00	
16:00	
17:00	**Today's self care**
18:00	
19:00	
20:00	**Chart your cycle**
21:00	
22:00	
23:00	**Positive affirmation**
Notes	

Friday | 21 February 2025 - Waning Crescent

6:00	Today's quick wins	
7:00		
8:00		
9:00		
10:00		
11:00	Health and nutrition	
12:00		
13:00		
14:00	Today, I am grateful for...	
15:00		
16:00		
17:00	Today's self care	
18:00		
19:00		
20:00	Chart your cycle	
21:00		
22:00		
23:00	Positive affirmation	
Notes		

Saturday | 22 February 2025 - Waning Crescent

6:00	**Today's quick wins**
7:00	
8:00	
9:00	
10:00	
11:00	**Health and nutrition**
12:00	
13:00	
14:00	**Today, I am grateful for...**
15:00	
16:00	
17:00	**Today's self care**
18:00	
19:00	
20:00	**Chart your cycle**
21:00	
22:00	
23:00	**Positive affirmation**
Notes	

Sunday | 23 February 2025 - Waning Crescent

6:00	**Today's quick wins**
7:00	
8:00	
9:00	
10:00	
11:00	**Health and nutrition**
12:00	
13:00	
14:00	**Today, I am grateful for...**
15:00	
16:00	
17:00	**Today's self care**
18:00	
19:00	
20:00	**Chart your cycle**
21:00	
22:00	
23:00	**Positive affirmation**
Notes	

Monday | 24 February 2025 - Waning Crescent

6:00		Today's quick wins
7:00		
8:00		
9:00		
10:00		
11:00		Health and nutrition
12:00		
13:00		
14:00		Today, I am grateful for...
15:00		
16:00		
17:00		Today's self care
18:00		
19:00		
20:00		Chart your cycle
21:00		
22:00		
23:00		Positive affirmation
Notes		

Tuesday | 25 February 2025 - Waning Crescent

6:00		Today's quick wins	
7:00			
8:00			
9:00			
10:00			
11:00		Health and nutrition	
12:00			
13:00			
14:00		Today, I am grateful for...	
15:00			
16:00			
17:00		Today's self care	
18:00			
19:00			
20:00		Chart your cycle	
21:00			
22:00			
23:00		Positive affirmation	
Notes			

Wednesday | 26 February 2025 - Waning Crescent

6:00		Today's quick wins
7:00		
8:00		
9:00		
10:00		
11:00		Health and nutrition
12:00		
13:00		
14:00		Today, I am grateful for...
15:00		
16:00		
17:00		Today's self care
18:00		
19:00		
20:00		Chart your cycle
21:00		
22:00		
23:00		Positive affirmation
Notes		

Thursday | 27 February 2025 - Waning Crescent

6:00	Today's quick wins	
7:00		
8:00		
9:00		
10:00		
11:00	Health and nutrition	
12:00		
13:00		
14:00	Today, I am grateful for…	
15:00		
16:00		
17:00	Today's self care	
18:00		
19:00		
20:00	Chart your cycle	
21:00		
22:00		
23:00	Positive affirmation	
Notes		

Friday | 28 February 2025 - New Moon in Pisces at 00.44 GMT

6:00		Today's quick wins
7:00		
8:00		
9:00		
10:00		
11:00		Health and nutrition
12:00		
13:00		
14:00		Today, I am grateful for…
15:00		
16:00		
17:00		Today's self care
18:00		
19:00		
20:00		Chart your cycle
21:00		
22:00		
23:00		Positive affirmation
Notes		

February achievements

Be proud of yourself and all that you have achieved this month. Write down your wins, big and small. If you have not achieved everything that you set out to do, that's okay! We learn and grow through our mistakes and experiences. You can use this space to make notes about anything that you have learned.

March 2025

Notes	Monday	Tuesday	Wednesday
	24	25	26
	3	4	5
	10	11	12
	17	18	19
	24 / 31	25	26

Thursday	Friday	Saturday	Sunday
27	28	1	2
6 ◐	7	8	9
13	14 ○	15	16
20 *Spring Equinox*	21	22 ◑	23
27	28	29 ●	30

March
Goddess Mami Wata

MAMI WATA

Mermaid goddess of healing, fertility and abundance.

A beautiful and enchanting goddess of West African roots. Revered in south east Nigeria.

Her symbol is the mirror. A portal between ocean and land allowing those that worship her to journey between realms.

She has power and influence over those who find themselves in her presence. Her followers wear red and white to symbolise her dual nature.
They use music to celebrate her, dancing as though in a trance. No one knows how far back she dates, but its possibly thousands of years, and today her figure is woven into popular culture in Africa and beyond.

Book: Mami Wata: Arts for Water Spirits in Africa and its Diasporas
Song: Goddess: Goddess Code by Lizzy Jeff
Moon phase: Waxing moon
Crystal: Unakite

My Vision for March

Saturday | 1 March 2025 - Waxing Crescent

6:00		Today's quick wins	
7:00			
8:00			
9:00			
10:00			
11:00		Health and nutrition	
12:00			
13:00			
14:00		Today, I am grateful for...	
15:00			
16:00			
17:00		Today's self care	
18:00			
19:00			
20:00		Chart your cycle	
21:00			
22:00			
23:00		Positive affirmation	
Notes			

Sunday | 2 March 2025 - Waxing Crescent

6:00		Today's quick wins	
7:00			
8:00			
9:00			
10:00			
11:00		Health and nutrition	
12:00			
13:00			
14:00		Today, I am grateful for...	
15:00			
16:00			
17:00		Today's self care	
18:00			
19:00			
20:00		Chart your cycle	
21:00			
22:00			
23:00		Positive affirmation	
Notes			

Monday | 3 March 2025 - Waxing Crescent

6:00	Today's quick wins	
7:00		
8:00		
9:00		
10:00		
11:00	Health and nutrition	
12:00		
13:00		
14:00	Today, I am grateful for…	
15:00		
16:00		
17:00	Today's self care	
18:00		
19:00		
20:00	Chart your cycle	
21:00		
22:00		
23:00	Positive affirmation	
Notes		

Tuesday | 4 March 2025 - Waxing Crescent

6:00	**Today's quick wins**
7:00	
8:00	
9:00	
10:00	
11:00	**Health and nutrition**
12:00	
13:00	
14:00	**Today, I am grateful for...**
15:00	
16:00	
17:00	**Today's self care**
18:00	
19:00	
20:00	**Chart your cycle**
21:00	
22:00	
23:00	**Positive affirmation**
Notes	

Wednesday | 5 March 2025 - Waxing Crescent

6:00		Today's quick wins	
7:00			
8:00			
9:00			
10:00			
11:00		Health and nutrition	
12:00			
13:00			
14:00		Today, I am grateful for…	
15:00			
16:00			
17:00		Today's self care	
18:00			
19:00			
20:00		Chart your cycle	
21:00			
22:00			
23:00		Positive affirmation	
Notes			

Thursday | 6 March 2025 - First Quarter

6:00		Today's quick wins
7:00		
8:00		
9:00		
10:00		
11:00		Health and nutrition
12:00		
13:00		
14:00		Today, I am grateful for...
15:00		
16:00		
17:00		Today's self care
18:00		
19:00		
20:00		Chart your cycle
21:00		
22:00		
23:00		Positive affirmation
Notes		

Friday | 7 March 2025 - Waxing Gibbous

6:00	Today's quick wins	
7:00		
8:00		
9:00		
10:00		
11:00	Health and nutrition	
12:00		
13:00		
14:00	Today, I am grateful for…	
15:00		
16:00		
17:00	Today's self care	
18:00		
19:00		
20:00	Chart your cycle	
21:00		
22:00		
23:00	Positive affirmation	
Notes		

Saturday | 8 March 2025 - Waxing Gibbous

6:00		**Today's quick wins**	
7:00			
8:00			
9:00			
10:00			
11:00		**Health and nutrition**	
12:00			
13:00			
14:00		**Today, I am grateful for...**	
15:00			
16:00			
17:00		**Today's self care**	
18:00			
19:00			
20:00		**Chart your cycle**	
21:00			
22:00			
23:00		**Positive affirmation**	
Notes			

Sunday | 9 March 2025 - Waxing Gibbous

6:00	**Today's quick wins**
7:00	
8:00	
9:00	
10:00	
11:00	**Health and nutrition**
12:00	
13:00	
14:00	**Today, I am grateful for…**
15:00	
16:00	
17:00	**Today's self care**
18:00	
19:00	
20:00	**Chart your cycle**
21:00	
22:00	
23:00	**Positive affirmation**
Notes	

Monday | 10 March 2025 - Waxing Gibbous

6:00	Today's quick wins	
7:00		
8:00		
9:00		
10:00		
11:00	Health and nutrition	
12:00		
13:00		
14:00	Today, I am grateful for…	
15:00		
16:00		
17:00	Today's self care	
18:00		
19:00		
20:00	Chart your cycle	
21:00		
22:00		
23:00	Positive affirmation	
Notes		

Tuesday | 11 March 2025 - Waxing Gibbous

6:00		Today's quick wins
7:00		
8:00		
9:00		
10:00		
11:00		Health and nutrition
12:00		
13:00		
14:00		Today, I am grateful for...
15:00		
16:00		
17:00		Today's self care
18:00		
19:00		
20:00		Chart your cycle
21:00		
22:00		
23:00		Positive affirmation
Notes		

Wednesday | 12 March 2025 - Waxing Gibbous

6:00	Today's quick wins	
7:00		
8:00		
9:00		
10:00		
11:00	Health and nutrition	
12:00		
13:00		
14:00	Today, I am grateful for...	
15:00		
16:00		
17:00	Today's self care	
18:00		
19:00		
20:00	Chart your cycle	
21:00		
22:00		
23:00	Positive affirmation	
Notes		

Thursday | 13 March 2025 - Waxing Gibbous

6:00		Today's quick wins	
7:00			
8:00			
9:00			
10:00			
11:00		Health and nutrition	
12:00			
13:00			
14:00		Today, I am grateful for...	
15:00			
16:00			
17:00		Today's self care	
18:00			
19:00			
20:00		Chart your cycle	
21:00			
22:00			
23:00		Positive affirmation	
Notes			

Friday | 14 March 2025 - Full Moon Lunar Eclipse in Virgo
06.54 GMT Moon moves to libra at 18.59

6:00	Today's quick wins
7:00	
8:00	
9:00	
10:00	
11:00	Health and nutrition
12:00	
13:00	
14:00	Today, I am grateful for...
15:00	
16:00	
17:00	Today's self care
18:00	
19:00	
20:00	Chart your cycle
21:00	
22:00	
23:00	Positive affirmation
Notes	

Saturday | 15 March 2025 - Waning Gibbous

6:00	Today's quick wins	
7:00		
8:00		
9:00		
10:00		
11:00	Health and nutrition	
12:00		
13:00		
14:00	Today, I am grateful for…	
15:00		
16:00		
17:00	Today's self care	
18:00		
19:00		
20:00	Chart your cycle	
21:00		
22:00		
23:00	Positive affirmation	
Notes		

Sunday | 16 March 2025 - Waning Gibbous

6:00	**Today's quick wins**
7:00	
8:00	
9:00	
10:00	
11:00	**Health and nutrition**
12:00	
13:00	
14:00	**Today, I am grateful for…**
15:00	
16:00	
17:00	**Today's self care**
18:00	
19:00	
20:00	**Chart your cycle**
21:00	
22:00	
23:00	**Positive affirmation**
Notes	

Monday | 17 March 2025 - Waning Gibbous

6:00		Today's quick wins	
7:00			
8:00			
9:00			
10:00			
11:00		Health and nutrition	
12:00			
13:00			
14:00		Today, I am grateful for...	
15:00			
16:00			
17:00		Today's self care	
18:00			
19:00			
20:00		Chart your cycle	
21:00			
22:00			
23:00		Positive affirmation	
Notes			

Tuesday | 18 March 2025 - Waning Gibbous

6:00		Today's quick wins
7:00		
8:00		
9:00		
10:00		
11:00		Health and nutrition
12:00		
13:00		
14:00		Today, I am grateful for...
15:00		
16:00		
17:00		Today's self care
18:00		
19:00		
20:00		Chart your cycle
21:00		
22:00		
23:00		Positive affirmation
Notes		

Wednesday | 19 March 2025 - Waning Gibbous

6:00		Today's quick wins
7:00		
8:00		
9:00		
10:00		
11:00		Health and nutrition
12:00		
13:00		
14:00		Today, I am grateful for...
15:00		
16:00		
17:00		Today's self care
18:00		
19:00		
20:00		Chart your cycle
21:00		
22:00		
23:00		Positive affirmation
Notes		

Thursday | 20 March 2025 - Waning Gibbous
Spring Equinox

6:00	Today's quick wins
7:00	
8:00	
9:00	
10:00	
11:00	Health and nutrition
12:00	
13:00	
14:00	Today, I am grateful for...
15:00	
16:00	
17:00	Today's self care
18:00	
19:00	
20:00	Chart your cycle
21:00	
22:00	
23:00	Positive affirmation
Notes	

Friday | 21 March 2025 - Waning Gibbous

6:00		Today's quick wins	
7:00			
8:00			
9:00			
10:00			
11:00		Health and nutrition	
12:00			
13:00			
14:00		Today, I am grateful for…	
15:00			
16:00			
17:00		Today's self care	
18:00			
19:00			
20:00		Chart your cycle	
21:00			
22:00			
23:00		Positive affirmation	
Notes			

Saturday | 22 March 2025 - Last Quarter

6:00	Today's quick wins
7:00	
8:00	
9:00	
10:00	
11:00	Health and nutrition
12:00	
13:00	
14:00	Today, I am grateful for...
15:00	
16:00	
17:00	Today's self care
18:00	
19:00	
20:00	Chart your cycle
21:00	
22:00	
23:00	Positive affirmation
Notes	

Sunday | 23 March 2025 - Waning Crescent

6:00	Today's quick wins
7:00	
8:00	
9:00	
10:00	
11:00	Health and nutrition
12:00	
13:00	
14:00	Today, I am grateful for...
15:00	
16:00	
17:00	Today's self care
18:00	
19:00	
20:00	Chart your cycle
21:00	
22:00	
23:00	Positive affirmation
Notes	

Monday | 24 March 2025 - Waning Crescent

6:00	**Today's quick wins**
7:00	
8:00	
9:00	
10:00	
11:00	**Health and nutrition**
12:00	
13:00	
14:00	**Today, I am grateful for...**
15:00	
16:00	
17:00	**Today's self care**
18:00	
19:00	
20:00	**Chart your cycle**
21:00	
22:00	
23:00	**Positive affirmation**
Notes	

Tuesday | 25 March 2025 - Waning Crescent

6:00		Today's quick wins	
7:00			
8:00			
9:00			
10:00			
11:00		Health and nutrition	
12:00			
13:00			
14:00		Today, I am grateful for...	
15:00			
16:00			
17:00		Today's self care	
18:00			
19:00			
20:00		Chart your cycle	
21:00			
22:00			
23:00		Positive affirmation	
Notes			

Wednesday | 26 March 2025 - Waning Crescent

6:00		Today's quick wins	
7:00			
8:00			
9:00			
10:00			
11:00		Health and nutrition	
12:00			
13:00			
14:00		Today, I am grateful for...	
15:00			
16:00			
17:00		Today's self care	
18:00			
19:00			
20:00		Chart your cycle	
21:00			
22:00			
23:00		Positive affirmation	
Notes			

Thursday | 27 March 2025 - Waning Crescent

6:00		Today's quick wins	
7:00			
8:00			
9:00			
10:00			
11:00		Health and nutrition	
12:00			
13:00			
14:00		Today, I am grateful for…	
15:00			
16:00			
17:00		Today's self care	
18:00			
19:00			
20:00		Chart your cycle	
21:00			
22:00			
23:00		Positive affirmation	
Notes			

Friday | 28 March 2025 - Waning Crescent

6:00	Today's quick wins	
7:00		
8:00		
9:00		
10:00		
11:00	Health and nutrition	
12:00		
13:00		
14:00	Today, I am grateful for…	
15:00		
16:00		
17:00	Today's self care	
18:00		
19:00		
20:00	Chart your cycle	
21:00		
22:00		
23:00	Positive affirmation	
Notes		

Saturday | 29 March 2025 - New Moon Solar Eclipse in Aries
10.57 GMT

6:00	Today's quick wins
7:00	
8:00	
9:00	
10:00	
11:00	Health and nutrition
12:00	
13:00	
14:00	Today, I am grateful for…
15:00	
16:00	
17:00	Today's self care
18:00	
19:00	
20:00	Chart your cycle
21:00	
22:00	
23:00	Positive affirmation
Notes	

Sunday | 30 March 2025 - Waxing Crescent

6:00	Today's quick wins	
7:00		
8:00		
9:00		
10:00		
11:00	Health and nutrition	
12:00		
13:00		
14:00	Today, I am grateful for...	
15:00		
16:00		
17:00	Today's self care	
18:00		
19:00		
20:00	Chart your cycle	
21:00		
22:00		
23:00	Positive affirmation	
Notes		

Monday | 31 March 2025 - Waxing Crescent

6:00		Today's quick wins
7:00		
8:00		
9:00		
10:00		
11:00		Health and nutrition
12:00		
13:00		
14:00		Today, I am grateful for…
15:00		
16:00		
17:00		Today's self care
18:00		
19:00		
20:00		Chart your cycle
21:00		
22:00		
23:00		Positive affirmation
Notes		

March achievements

Be proud of yourself and all that you have achieved this month. Write down your wins, big and small. If you have not achieved everything that you set out to do, that's okay! We learn and grow through our mistakes and experiences. You can use this space to make notes about anything that you have learned.

April 2025

Notes	Monday	Tuesday	Wednesday
	31	1	2
	7	8	9
	14	15	16
	21	22	23
	28	29	30

Thursday	Friday	Saturday	Sunday
3	4	5 ☾	6
10	11	12	13 ○
17	18	19	20
24	25	26	27 ●
1	2	3	4

April
Goddess Nike

NIKE

Greek goddess of Victory.

She has a temple on the Acropolis which can still be visited today.

In ancient Greece temples to Nike doubled as communal spaces where victories in war and athletics were celebrated.

It has not gone unnoticed that the major corporations who have chosen to name their companies after goddesses have achieved great success. Testament to the power of the goddess in modernity.

Books: Shoe Dog by Phil Knight
Song: Manifestations by Peachkka
Moon phase: Full moon
Crystal: Aventurine

My Vision for April

Tuesday | 1 April 2025 - Waxing Crescent

6:00		Today's quick wins	
7:00			
8:00			
9:00			
10:00			
11:00		Health and nutrition	
12:00			
13:00			
14:00		Today, I am grateful for...	
15:00			
16:00			
17:00		Today's self care	
18:00			
19:00			
20:00		Chart your cycle	
21:00			
22:00			
23:00		Positive affirmation	
Notes			

Wednesday | 2 April 2025 - Waxing Crescent

6:00	Today's quick wins	
7:00		
8:00		
9:00		
10:00		
11:00	Health and nutrition	
12:00		
13:00		
14:00	Today, I am grateful for...	
15:00		
16:00		
17:00	Today's self care	
18:00		
19:00		
20:00	Chart your cycle	
21:00		
22:00		
23:00	Positive affirmation	
Notes		

Thursday | 3 April 2025 - Waxing Crescent

6:00		**Today's quick wins**
7:00		
8:00		
9:00		
10:00		
11:00		**Health and nutrition**
12:00		
13:00		
14:00		**Today, I am grateful for…**
15:00		
16:00		
17:00		**Today's self care**
18:00		
19:00		
20:00		**Chart your cycle**
21:00		
22:00		
23:00		**Positive affirmation**
Notes		

Friday | 4 April 2025 - Waxing Crescent

6:00	**Today's quick wins**
7:00	
8:00	
9:00	
10:00	
11:00	**Health and nutrition**
12:00	
13:00	
14:00	**Today, I am grateful for...**
15:00	
16:00	
17:00	**Today's self care**
18:00	
19:00	
20:00	**Chart your cycle**
21:00	
22:00	
23:00	**Positive affirmation**
Notes	

# Saturday | 5 April 2025 - First Quarter

6:00		Today's quick wins
7:00		
8:00		
9:00		
10:00		
11:00		Health and nutrition
12:00		
13:00		
14:00		Today, I am grateful for…
15:00		
16:00		
17:00		Today's self care
18:00		
19:00		
20:00		Chart your cycle
21:00		
22:00		
23:00		Positive affirmation
Notes		

Sunday | 6 April 2025 - Waxing Gibbous

6:00	**Today's quick wins**
7:00	
8:00	
9:00	
10:00	
11:00	**Health and nutrition**
12:00	
13:00	
14:00	**Today, I am grateful for...**
15:00	
16:00	
17:00	**Today's self care**
18:00	
19:00	
20:00	**Chart your cycle**
21:00	
22:00	
23:00	**Positive affirmation**
Notes	

Monday | 7 April 2025 - Waxing Gibbous

6:00		Today's quick wins	
7:00			
8:00			
9:00			
10:00			
11:00		Health and nutrition	
12:00			
13:00			
14:00		Today, I am grateful for...	
15:00			
16:00			
17:00		Today's self care	
18:00			
19:00			
20:00		Chart your cycle	
21:00			
22:00			
23:00		Positive affirmation	
Notes			

Tuesday | 8 April 2025 - Waxing Gibbous

6:00	**Today's quick wins**
7:00	
8:00	
9:00	
10:00	
11:00	**Health and nutrition**
12:00	
13:00	
14:00	**Today, I am grateful for...**
15:00	
16:00	
17:00	**Today's self care**
18:00	
19:00	
20:00	**Chart your cycle**
21:00	
22:00	
23:00	**Positive affirmation**
Notes	

Wednesday | 9 April 2025 - Waxing Gibbous

6:00		Today's quick wins	
7:00			
8:00			
9:00			
10:00			
11:00		Health and nutrition	
12:00			
13:00			
14:00		Today, I am grateful for…	
15:00			
16:00			
17:00		Today's self care	
18:00			
19:00			
20:00		Chart your cycle	
21:00			
22:00			
23:00		Positive affirmation	
Notes			

Thursday | 10 April 2025 - Waxing Gibbous

6:00		Today's quick wins	
7:00			
8:00			
9:00			
10:00			
11:00		Health and nutrition	
12:00			
13:00			
14:00		Today, I am grateful for...	
15:00			
16:00			
17:00		Today's self care	
18:00			
19:00			
20:00		Chart your cycle	
21:00			
22:00			
23:00		Positive affirmation	
Notes			

Friday | 11 April 2025 - Waxing Gibbous

6:00		Today's quick wins	
7:00			
8:00			
9:00			
10:00			
11:00		Health and nutrition	
12:00			
13:00			
14:00		Today, I am grateful for…	
15:00			
16:00			
17:00		Today's self care	
18:00			
19:00			
20:00		Chart your cycle	
21:00			
22:00			
23:00		Positive affirmation	
Notes			

Saturday | 12 April 2025 - Waxing Gibbous

6:00	Today's quick wins	
7:00		
8:00		
9:00		
10:00		
11:00	Health and nutrition	
12:00		
13:00		
14:00	Today, I am grateful for...	
15:00		
16:00		
17:00	Today's self care	
18:00		
19:00		
20:00	Chart your cycle	
21:00		
22:00		
23:00	Positive affirmation	
Notes		

Sunday | 13 April 2025 - Full Moon in Libra at 00.21 GMT *moves to Scorpio at 13.54*

6:00		Today's quick wins	
7:00			
8:00			
9:00			
10:00			
11:00		Health and nutrition	
12:00			
13:00			
14:00		Today, I am grateful for…	
15:00			
16:00			
17:00		Today's self care	
18:00			
19:00			
20:00		Chart your cycle	
21:00			
22:00			
23:00		Positive affirmation	
Notes			

Monday | 14 April 2025 - Waning Gibbous

6:00	Today's quick wins
7:00	
8:00	
9:00	
10:00	
11:00	Health and nutrition
12:00	
13:00	
14:00	Today, I am grateful for...
15:00	
16:00	
17:00	Today's self care
18:00	
19:00	
20:00	Chart your cycle
21:00	
22:00	
23:00	Positive affirmation
Notes	

Tuesday | 15 April 2025 - Waning Gibbous

6:00		Today's quick wins	
7:00			
8:00			
9:00			
10:00			
11:00		Health and nutrition	
12:00			
13:00			
14:00		Today, I am grateful for…	
15:00			
16:00			
17:00		Today's self care	
18:00			
19:00			
20:00		Chart your cycle	
21:00			
22:00			
23:00		Positive affirmation	
Notes			

Wednesday | 16 April 2025 - Waning Gibbous

6:00	Today's quick wins	
7:00		
8:00		
9:00		
10:00		
11:00	Health and nutrition	
12:00		
13:00		
14:00	Today, I am grateful for…	
15:00		
16:00		
17:00	Today's self care	
18:00		
19:00		
20:00	Chart your cycle	
21:00		
22:00		
23:00	Positive affirmation	
Notes		

Thursday | 17 April 2025 - Waning Gibbous

6:00		Today's quick wins	
7:00			
8:00			
9:00			
10:00			
11:00		Health and nutrition	
12:00			
13:00			
14:00		Today, I am grateful for…	
15:00			
16:00			
17:00		Today's self care	
18:00			
19:00			
20:00		Chart your cycle	
21:00			
22:00			
23:00		Positive affirmation	
Notes			

Friday | 18 April 2025 - Waning Gibbous

6:00	Today's quick wins	
7:00		
8:00		
9:00		
10:00		
11:00	Health and nutrition	
12:00		
13:00		
14:00	Today, I am grateful for...	
15:00		
16:00		
17:00	Today's self care	
18:00		
19:00		
20:00	Chart your cycle	
21:00		
22:00		
23:00	Positive affirmation	
Notes		

Saturday | 19 April 2025 - Waning Gibbous

6:00	**Today's quick wins**
7:00	
8:00	
9:00	
10:00	
11:00	**Health and nutrition**
12:00	
13:00	
14:00	**Today, I am grateful for...**
15:00	
16:00	
17:00	**Today's self care**
18:00	
19:00	
20:00	**Chart your cycle**
21:00	
22:00	
23:00	**Positive affirmation**
Notes	

Sunday | 20 April 2025 - Last Quarter

6:00	**Today's quick wins**
7:00	
8:00	
9:00	
10:00	
11:00	**Health and nutrition**
12:00	
13:00	
14:00	**Today, I am grateful for...**
15:00	
16:00	
17:00	**Today's self care**
18:00	
19:00	
20:00	**Chart your cycle**
21:00	
22:00	
23:00	**Positive affirmation**
Notes	

Monday | 21 April 2025 - Last Quarter

6:00		Today's quick wins
7:00		
8:00		
9:00		
10:00		
11:00		Health and nutrition
12:00		
13:00		
14:00		Today, I am grateful for…
15:00		
16:00		
17:00		Today's self care
18:00		
19:00		
20:00		Chart your cycle
21:00		
22:00		
23:00		Positive affirmation
Notes		

Tuesday | 22 April 2025 - Waning Crescent

6:00		Today's quick wins
7:00		
8:00		
9:00		
10:00		
11:00		Health and nutrition
12:00		
13:00		
14:00		Today, I am grateful for…
15:00		
16:00		
17:00		Today's self care
18:00		
19:00		
20:00		Chart your cycle
21:00		
22:00		
23:00		Positive affirmation
Notes		

Wednesday | 23 April 2025 - Waning Crescent

6:00	Today's quick wins
7:00	
8:00	
9:00	
10:00	
11:00	Health and nutrition
12:00	
13:00	
14:00	Today, I am grateful for...
15:00	
16:00	
17:00	Today's self care
18:00	
19:00	
20:00	Chart your cycle
21:00	
22:00	
23:00	Positive affirmation
Notes	

Thursday | 24 April 2025 - Waning Crescent

6:00	Today's quick wins
7:00	
8:00	
9:00	
10:00	
11:00	Health and nutrition
12:00	
13:00	
14:00	Today, I am grateful for...
15:00	
16:00	
17:00	Today's self care
18:00	
19:00	
20:00	Chart your cycle
21:00	
22:00	
23:00	Positive affirmation
Notes	

Friday | 25 April 2025 - Waning Crescent

6:00	Today's quick wins	
7:00		
8:00		
9:00		
10:00		
11:00	Health and nutrition	
12:00		
13:00		
14:00	Today, I am grateful for…	
15:00		
16:00		
17:00	Today's self care	
18:00		
19:00		
20:00	Chart your cycle	
21:00		
22:00		
23:00	Positive affirmation	
Notes		

Saturday | 26 April 2025 - Waning Crescent

6:00	Today's quick wins	
7:00		
8:00		
9:00		
10:00		
11:00	Health and nutrition	
12:00		
13:00		
14:00	Today, I am grateful for…	
15:00		
16:00		
17:00	Today's self care	
18:00		
19:00		
20:00	Chart your cycle	
21:00		
22:00		
23:00	Positive affirmation	
Notes		

Sunday | 27 April 2025 - New Moon in Taurus at 19.30 GMT

6:00	Today's quick wins	
7:00		
8:00		
9:00		
10:00		
11:00	Health and nutrition	
12:00		
13:00		
14:00	Today, I am grateful for…	
15:00		
16:00		
17:00	Today's self care	
18:00		
19:00		
20:00	Chart your cycle	
21:00		
22:00		
23:00	Positive affirmation	
Notes		

Monday | 28 April 2025 - Waxing Crescent

6:00	Today's quick wins	
7:00		
8:00		
9:00		
10:00		
11:00	Health and nutrition	
12:00		
13:00		
14:00	Today, I am grateful for...	
15:00		
16:00		
17:00	Today's self care	
18:00		
19:00		
20:00	Chart your cycle	
21:00		
22:00		
23:00	Positive affirmation	
Notes		

Tuesday | 29 April 2025 - Waxing Crescent

6:00	Today's quick wins	
7:00		
8:00		
9:00		
10:00		
11:00	Health and nutrition	
12:00		
13:00		
14:00	Today, I am grateful for…	
15:00		
16:00		
17:00	Today's self care	
18:00		
19:00		
20:00	Chart your cycle	
21:00		
22:00		
23:00	Positive affirmation	
Notes		

Wednesday | 30 April 2025 - Waxing Crescent

6:00	**Today's quick wins**
7:00	
8:00	
9:00	
10:00	
11:00	**Health and nutrition**
12:00	
13:00	
14:00	**Today, I am grateful for...**
15:00	
16:00	
17:00	**Today's self care**
18:00	
19:00	
20:00	**Chart your cycle**
21:00	
22:00	
23:00	**Positive affirmation**
Notes	

April achievements

Be proud of yourself and all that you have achieved this month. Write down your wins, big and small. If you have not achieved everything that you set out to do, that's okay! We learn and grow through our mistakes and experiences. You can use this space to make notes about anything that you have learned.

"Work in the invisible world at least as hard as you do in the visible."
—Rumi

May 2025

Notes	Monday	Tuesday	Wednesday
	28	29	30
	5	6	7
	12 ○	13	14
	19	20 ☾	21
	26	27 ●	28

Thursday	Friday	Saturday	Sunday
1	2	3	4
8	9	10	11
15	16	17	18
22	23	24	25
29	30	31	

May
Goddess Artemis

ARTEMIS

Greek goddess of hunting, wilderness, the moon, nature and childbirth.

A free spirit and lover of the wilderness. Forever a maiden since she swore not to marry.

Artemis was a skilled hunter, but she also treated animals with love and respect. She protected and honoured them.

She embodies beauty and adventure. Artists and poets love her. Artemis is often depicted dancing in rivers and forests with nymphs. She was even said to be Shakespeare's favourite since he references her so often.

Books: Awakening Artemis by Vanessa Chakour
Songs: Howl at the Moon by Nidala
Crystal: Moss Agate
Moon phase: Full moon

My Vision for May

Thursday | 1 May 2025 - Waxing Crescent

6:00	Today's quick wins	
7:00		
8:00		
9:00		
10:00		
11:00	Health and nutrition	
12:00		
13:00		
14:00	Today, I am grateful for...	
15:00		
16:00		
17:00	Today's self care	
18:00		
19:00		
20:00	Chart your cycle	
21:00		
22:00		
23:00	Positive affirmation	
Notes		

Friday | 2 May 2025 - Waxing Crescent

6:00	Today's quick wins
7:00	
8:00	
9:00	
10:00	
11:00	Health and nutrition
12:00	
13:00	
14:00	Today, I am grateful for...
15:00	
16:00	
17:00	Today's self care
18:00	
19:00	
20:00	Chart your cycle
21:00	
22:00	
23:00	Positive affirmation
Notes	

Saturday | 3 May 2025 - Waxing Crescent

6:00		Today's quick wins	
7:00			
8:00			
9:00			
10:00			
11:00		Health and nutrition	
12:00			
13:00			
14:00		Today, I am grateful for…	
15:00			
16:00			
17:00		Today's self care	
18:00			
19:00			
20:00		Chart your cycle	
21:00			
22:00			
23:00		Positive affirmation	
Notes			

Sunday | 4 May 2025 - First Quarter

6:00		Today's quick wins	
7:00			
8:00			
9:00			
10:00			
11:00		Health and nutrition	
12:00			
13:00			
14:00		Today, I am grateful for...	
15:00			
16:00			
17:00		Today's self care	
18:00			
19:00			
20:00		Chart your cycle	
21:00			
22:00			
23:00		Positive affirmation	
Notes			

Monday | 5 May 2025 - Waxing Gibbous

6:00		Today's quick wins	
7:00			
8:00			
9:00			
10:00			
11:00		Health and nutrition	
12:00			
13:00			
14:00		Today, I am grateful for...	
15:00			
16:00			
17:00		Today's self care	
18:00			
19:00			
20:00		Chart your cycle	
21:00			
22:00			
23:00		Positive affirmation	
Notes			

Tuesday | 6 May 2025 - Waxing Gibbous

6:00	Today's quick wins	
7:00		
8:00		
9:00		
10:00		
11:00	Health and nutrition	
12:00		
13:00		
14:00	Today, I am grateful for...	
15:00		
16:00		
17:00	Today's self care	
18:00		
19:00		
20:00	Chart your cycle	
21:00		
22:00		
23:00	Positive affirmation	
Notes		

Wednesday | 7 May 2025 - Waxing Gibbous

6:00	**Today's quick wins**
7:00	
8:00	
9:00	
10:00	
11:00	**Health and nutrition**
12:00	
13:00	
14:00	**Today, I am grateful for…**
15:00	
16:00	
17:00	**Today's self care**
18:00	
19:00	
20:00	**Chart your cycle**
21:00	
22:00	
23:00	**Positive affirmation**
Notes	

Thursday | 8 May 2025 - Waxing Gibbous

6:00	Today's quick wins	
7:00		
8:00		
9:00		
10:00		
11:00	Health and nutrition	
12:00		
13:00		
14:00	Today, I am grateful for...	
15:00		
16:00		
17:00	Today's self care	
18:00		
19:00		
20:00	Chart your cycle	
21:00		
22:00		
23:00	Positive affirmation	
Notes		

Friday | 9 May 2025 - Waxing Gibbous

6:00		Today's quick wins	
7:00			
8:00			
9:00			
10:00			
11:00		Health and nutrition	
12:00			
13:00			
14:00		Today, I am grateful for...	
15:00			
16:00			
17:00		Today's self care	
18:00			
19:00			
20:00		Chart your cycle	
21:00			
22:00			
23:00		Positive affirmation	
Notes			

Saturday | 10 May 2025 - Waxing Gibbous

6:00	Today's quick wins	
7:00		
8:00		
9:00		
10:00		
11:00	Health and nutrition	
12:00		
13:00		
14:00	Today, I am grateful for...	
15:00		
16:00		
17:00	Today's self care	
18:00		
19:00		
20:00	Chart your cycle	
21:00		
22:00		
23:00	Positive affirmation	
Notes		

Sunday | 11 May 2025 - Waxing Gibbous

6:00	**Today's quick wins**
7:00	
8:00	
9:00	
10:00	
11:00	**Health and nutrition**
12:00	
13:00	
14:00	**Today, I am grateful for…**
15:00	
16:00	
17:00	**Today's self care**
18:00	
19:00	
20:00	**Chart your cycle**
21:00	
22:00	
23:00	**Positive affirmation**
Notes	

Monday | 12 May 2025 - Full Moon in Scorpio 16:55 GMT

6:00	Today's quick wins	
7:00		
8:00		
9:00		
10:00		
11:00	Health and nutrition	
12:00		
13:00		
14:00	Today, I am grateful for...	
15:00		
16:00		
17:00	Today's self care	
18:00		
19:00		
20:00	Chart your cycle	
21:00		
22:00		
23:00	Positive affirmation	
Notes		

Tuesday | 13 May 2025 - Waning Gibbous

6:00		Today's quick wins	
7:00			
8:00			
9:00			
10:00			
11:00		Health and nutrition	
12:00			
13:00			
14:00		Today, I am grateful for…	
15:00			
16:00			
17:00		Today's self care	
18:00			
19:00			
20:00		Chart your cycle	
21:00			
22:00			
23:00		Positive affirmation	
Notes			

Wednesday | 14 May 2025 - Waning Gibbous

6:00	Today's quick wins	
7:00		
8:00		
9:00		
10:00		
11:00	Health and nutrition	
12:00		
13:00		
14:00	Today, I am grateful for…	
15:00		
16:00		
17:00	Today's self care	
18:00		
19:00		
20:00	Chart your cycle	
21:00		
22:00		
23:00	Positive affirmation	
Notes		

Thursday | 15 May 2025 - Waning Gibbous

6:00		Today's quick wins	
7:00			
8:00			
9:00			
10:00			
11:00		Health and nutrition	
12:00			
13:00			
14:00		Today, I am grateful for…	
15:00			
16:00			
17:00		Today's self care	
18:00			
19:00			
20:00		Chart your cycle	
21:00			
22:00			
23:00		Positive affirmation	
Notes			

Friday | 16 May 2025 - Waning Gibbous

6:00	**Today's quick wins**
7:00	
8:00	
9:00	
10:00	
11:00	**Health and nutrition**
12:00	
13:00	
14:00	**Today, I am grateful for…**
15:00	
16:00	
17:00	**Today's self care**
18:00	
19:00	
20:00	**Chart your cycle**
21:00	
22:00	
23:00	**Positive affirmation**
Notes	

Saturday | 17 May 2025 - Waning Gibbous

6:00	Today's quick wins
7:00	
8:00	
9:00	
10:00	
11:00	Health and nutrition
12:00	
13:00	
14:00	Today, I am grateful for…
15:00	
16:00	
17:00	Today's self care
18:00	
19:00	
20:00	Chart your cycle
21:00	
22:00	
23:00	Positive affirmation
Notes	

Sunday | 18 May 2025 - Waning Gibbous

6:00	**Today's quick wins**
7:00	
8:00	
9:00	
10:00	
11:00	**Health and nutrition**
12:00	
13:00	
14:00	**Today, I am grateful for...**
15:00	
16:00	
17:00	**Today's self care**
18:00	
19:00	
20:00	**Chart your cycle**
21:00	
22:00	
23:00	**Positive affirmation**
Notes	

> # Monday | 19 May 2025 - Waning Gibbous

6:00		Today's quick wins
7:00		
8:00		
9:00		
10:00		
11:00		Health and nutrition
12:00		
13:00		
14:00		Today, I am grateful for...
15:00		
16:00		
17:00		Today's self care
18:00		
19:00		
20:00		Chart your cycle
21:00		
22:00		
23:00		Positive affirmation
Notes		

Tuesday | 20 May 2025 - Last Quarter

6:00	**Today's quick wins**
7:00	
8:00	
9:00	
10:00	
11:00	**Health and nutrition**
12:00	
13:00	
14:00	**Today, I am grateful for...**
15:00	
16:00	
17:00	**Today's self care**
18:00	
19:00	
20:00	**Chart your cycle**
21:00	
22:00	
23:00	**Positive affirmation**
Notes	

Wednesday | 21 May 2025 - Waning Crescent

6:00		Today's quick wins	
7:00			
8:00			
9:00			
10:00			
11:00		Health and nutrition	
12:00			
13:00			
14:00		Today, I am grateful for…	
15:00			
16:00			
17:00		Today's self care	
18:00			
19:00			
20:00		Chart your cycle	
21:00			
22:00			
23:00		Positive affirmation	
Notes			

Thursday | 22 May 2025 - Waning Crescent

6:00		**Today's quick wins**
7:00		
8:00		
9:00		
10:00		
11:00		**Health and nutrition**
12:00		
13:00		
14:00		**Today, I am grateful for…**
15:00		
16:00		
17:00		**Today's self care**
18:00		
19:00		
20:00		**Chart your cycle**
21:00		
22:00		
23:00		**Positive affirmation**
Notes		

Friday | 23 May 2025 - Waning Crescent

6:00	Today's quick wins	
7:00		
8:00		
9:00		
10:00		
11:00	Health and nutrition	
12:00		
13:00		
14:00	Today, I am grateful for...	
15:00		
16:00		
17:00	Today's self care	
18:00		
19:00		
20:00	Chart your cycle	
21:00		
22:00		
23:00	Positive affirmation	
Notes		

Saturday | 24 May 2025 - Waning Crescent

6:00	**Today's quick wins**
7:00	
8:00	
9:00	
10:00	
11:00	**Health and nutrition**
12:00	
13:00	
14:00	**Today, I am grateful for...**
15:00	
16:00	
17:00	**Today's self care**
18:00	
19:00	
20:00	**Chart your cycle**
21:00	
22:00	
23:00	**Positive affirmation**
Notes	

Sunday | 25 May 2025 - Waning Crescent

6:00	Today's quick wins
7:00	
8:00	
9:00	
10:00	
11:00	Health and nutrition
12:00	
13:00	
14:00	Today, I am grateful for...
15:00	
16:00	
17:00	Today's self care
18:00	
19:00	
20:00	Chart your cycle
21:00	
22:00	
23:00	Positive affirmation
Notes	

Monday | 26 May 2025 - Waning Crescent

6:00	Today's quick wins	
7:00		
8:00		
9:00		
10:00		
11:00	Health and nutrition	
12:00		
13:00		
14:00	Today, I am grateful for...	
15:00		
16:00		
17:00	Today's self care	
18:00		
19:00		
20:00	Chart your cycle	
21:00		
22:00		
23:00	Positive affirmation	
Notes		

Tuesday | 27 May 2025 - New Moon in Gemini at 03.02 GMT

6:00	Today's quick wins	
7:00		
8:00		
9:00		
10:00		
11:00	Health and nutrition	
12:00		
13:00		
14:00	Today, I am grateful for…	
15:00		
16:00		
17:00	Today's self care	
18:00		
19:00		
20:00	Chart your cycle	
21:00		
22:00		
23:00	Positive affirmation	
Notes		

Wednesday | 28 May 2025 - Waxing Crescent

6:00		Today's quick wins	
7:00			
8:00			
9:00			
10:00			
11:00		Health and nutrition	
12:00			
13:00			
14:00		Today, I am grateful for...	
15:00			
16:00			
17:00		Today's self care	
18:00			
19:00			
20:00		Chart your cycle	
21:00			
22:00			
23:00		Positive affirmation	
Notes			

Thursday | 29 May 2025 - Waxing Crescent

6:00	Today's quick wins	
7:00		
8:00		
9:00		
10:00		
11:00	Health and nutrition	
12:00		
13:00		
14:00	Today, I am grateful for…	
15:00		
16:00		
17:00	Today's self care	
18:00		
19:00		
20:00	Chart your cycle	
21:00		
22:00		
23:00	Positive affirmation	
Notes		

Friday | 30 May 2025 - Waxing Crescent

6:00		Today's quick wins	
7:00			
8:00			
9:00			
10:00			
11:00		Health and nutrition	
12:00			
13:00			
14:00		Today, I am grateful for…	
15:00			
16:00			
17:00		Today's self care	
18:00			
19:00			
20:00		Chart your cycle	
21:00			
22:00			
23:00		Positive affirmation	
Notes			

Saturday | 31 May 2025 - Waxing Crescent

6:00		Today's quick wins
7:00		
8:00		
9:00		
10:00		
11:00		Health and nutrition
12:00		
13:00		
14:00		Today, I am grateful for…
15:00		
16:00		
17:00		Today's self care
18:00		
19:00		
20:00		Chart your cycle
21:00		
22:00		
23:00		Positive affirmation
Notes		

May achievements

Be proud of yourself and all that you have achieved this month. Write down your wins, big and small. If you have not achieved everything that you set out to do, that's okay! We learn and grow through our mistakes and experiences. You can use this space to make notes about anything that you have learned.

June 2025

Notes	Monday	Tuesday	Wednesday
	26	27	28
	2	3	4
	9	10	11
	16	17	18
	23	24	25
	30		

Thursday	Friday	Saturday	Sunday
29	30	31	1
5	6	7	8
12	13	14	15
19	20	21 *Summer Solstice*	22
26	27	28	29

June
Goddess Juno

JUNO

Goddess of Marriage and Childbirth,
Mother of Rome and Protector of Women.

Juno Moneta refers to the goddess of Rome that was the protector of funds. In the Temple of Juno Moneta, the first Roman coins were minted and continued to be minted there for over four centuries.

Festivals throughout the year were connected to the waxing and waning moons. It was believed that Juno controlled the cycles of the moon and seasons. The month of June was named in her honour. The peacock, lion and cuckoos serve as her sacred animals.

Books: Childbirth as a Rite of Passage by Dr Rachel Reed
Song: We are Rising by Mary Isis
Crystal: Rose Quartz
Moon phase: Waxing and Waning moon

My Vision for June

Sunday | 1 June 2025 - Waxing Crescent

6:00	**Today's quick wins**
7:00	
8:00	
9:00	
10:00	
11:00	**Health and nutrition**
12:00	
13:00	
14:00	**Today, I am grateful for…**
15:00	
16:00	
17:00	**Today's self care**
18:00	
19:00	
20:00	**Chart your cycle**
21:00	
22:00	
23:00	**Positive affirmation**
Notes	

Monday | 2 June 2025 - Waxing Crescent

6:00	**Today's quick wins**
7:00	
8:00	
9:00	
10:00	
11:00	**Health and nutrition**
12:00	
13:00	
14:00	**Today, I am grateful for...**
15:00	
16:00	
17:00	**Today's self care**
18:00	
19:00	
20:00	**Chart your cycle**
21:00	
22:00	
23:00	**Positive affirmation**
Notes	

Tuesday | 3 June 2025 - First Quarter

6:00		Today's quick wins
7:00		
8:00		
9:00		
10:00		
11:00		Health and nutrition
12:00		
13:00		
14:00		Today, I am grateful for...
15:00		
16:00		
17:00		Today's self care
18:00		
19:00		
20:00		Chart your cycle
21:00		
22:00		
23:00		Positive affirmation
Notes		

Wednesday | 4 June 2025 - Waxing Gibbous

6:00	**Today's quick wins**	
7:00		
8:00		
9:00		
10:00		
11:00	**Health and nutrition**	
12:00		
13:00		
14:00	**Today, I am grateful for…**	
15:00		
16:00		
17:00	**Today's self care**	
18:00		
19:00		
20:00	**Chart your cycle**	
21:00		
22:00		
23:00	**Positive affirmation**	
Notes		

Thursday | 5 June 2025 - Waxing Gibbous

6:00		Today's quick wins	
7:00			
8:00			
9:00			
10:00			
11:00		Health and nutrition	
12:00			
13:00			
14:00		Today, I am grateful for...	
15:00			
16:00			
17:00		Today's self care	
18:00			
19:00			
20:00		Chart your cycle	
21:00			
22:00			
23:00		Positive affirmation	
Notes			

Friday | 6 June 2025 - Waxing Gibbous

6:00		Today's quick wins	
7:00			
8:00			
9:00			
10:00			
11:00		Health and nutrition	
12:00			
13:00			
14:00		Today, I am grateful for...	
15:00			
16:00			
17:00		Today's self care	
18:00			
19:00			
20:00		Chart your cycle	
21:00			
22:00			
23:00		Positive affirmation	
Notes			

Saturday | 7 June 2025 - Waxing Gibbous

6:00	**Today's quick wins**
7:00	
8:00	
9:00	
10:00	
11:00	**Health and nutrition**
12:00	
13:00	
14:00	**Today, I am grateful for...**
15:00	
16:00	
17:00	**Today's self care**
18:00	
19:00	
20:00	**Chart your cycle**
21:00	
22:00	
23:00	**Positive affirmation**
Notes	

Sunday | 8 June 2025 - Waxing Gibbous

6:00	Today's quick wins	
7:00		
8:00		
9:00		
10:00		
11:00	Health and nutrition	
12:00		
13:00		
14:00	Today, I am grateful for...	
15:00		
16:00		
17:00	Today's self care	
18:00		
19:00		
20:00	Chart your cycle	
21:00		
22:00		
23:00	Positive affirmation	
Notes		

Monday | 9 June 2025 - Waxing Gibbous

6:00	Today's quick wins	
7:00		
8:00		
9:00		
10:00		
11:00	Health and nutrition	
12:00		
13:00		
14:00	Today, I am grateful for...	
15:00		
16:00		
17:00	Today's self care	
18:00		
19:00		
20:00	Chart your cycle	
21:00		
22:00		
23:00	Positive affirmation	
Notes		

Tuesday | 10 June 2025 - Waxing Gibbous

6:00		**Today's quick wins**	
7:00			
8:00			
9:00			
10:00			
11:00		**Health and nutrition**	
12:00			
13:00			
14:00		**Today, I am grateful for…**	
15:00			
16:00			
17:00		**Today's self care**	
18:00			
19:00			
20:00		**Chart your cycle**	
21:00			
22:00			
23:00		**Positive affirmation**	
Notes			

Wednesday | 11 June 2025 - Full Moon in Sagittarius at 07.43 GMT

6:00		Today's quick wins
7:00		
8:00		
9:00		
10:00		
11:00		Health and nutrition
12:00		
13:00		
14:00		Today, I am grateful for…
15:00		
16:00		
17:00		Today's self care
18:00		
19:00		
20:00		Chart your cycle
21:00		
22:00		
23:00		Positive affirmation
Notes		

Thursday | 12 June 2025 - Waning Gibbous

6:00	Today's quick wins	
7:00		
8:00		
9:00		
10:00		
11:00	Health and nutrition	
12:00		
13:00		
14:00	Today, I am grateful for…	
15:00		
16:00		
17:00	Today's self care	
18:00		
19:00		
20:00	Chart your cycle	
21:00		
22:00		
23:00	Positive affirmation	
Notes		

Friday | 13 June 2025 - Waning Gibbous

6:00		Today's quick wins
7:00		
8:00		
9:00		
10:00		
11:00		Health and nutrition
12:00		
13:00		
14:00		Today, I am grateful for...
15:00		
16:00		
17:00		Today's self care
18:00		
19:00		
20:00		Chart your cycle
21:00		
22:00		
23:00		Positive affirmation
Notes		

Saturday | 14 June 2025 - Waning Gibbous

6:00	**Today's quick wins**
7:00	
8:00	
9:00	
10:00	
11:00	**Health and nutrition**
12:00	
13:00	
14:00	**Today, I am grateful for…**
15:00	
16:00	
17:00	**Today's self care**
18:00	
19:00	
20:00	**Chart your cycle**
21:00	
22:00	
23:00	**Positive affirmation**
Notes	

Sunday | 15 June 2025 - Waning Gibbous

6:00	**Today's quick wins**
7:00	
8:00	
9:00	
10:00	
11:00	**Health and nutrition**
12:00	
13:00	
14:00	**Today, I am grateful for...**
15:00	
16:00	
17:00	**Today's self care**
18:00	
19:00	
20:00	**Chart your cycle**
21:00	
22:00	
23:00	**Positive affirmation**
Notes	

Monday | 16 June 2025 - Waning Gibbous

6:00		Today's quick wins
7:00		
8:00		
9:00		
10:00		
11:00		Health and nutrition
12:00		
13:00		
14:00		Today, I am grateful for…
15:00		
16:00		
17:00		Today's self care
18:00		
19:00		
20:00		Chart your cycle
21:00		
22:00		
23:00		Positive affirmation
Notes		

Tuesday | 17 June 2025 - Waning Gibbous

6:00		Today's quick wins
7:00		
8:00		
9:00		
10:00		
11:00		Health and nutrition
12:00		
13:00		
14:00		Today, I am grateful for...
15:00		
16:00		
17:00		Today's self care
18:00		
19:00		
20:00		Chart your cycle
21:00		
22:00		
23:00		Positive affirmation
Notes		

Wednesday | 18 June 2025 - Last Quarter

6:00	Today's quick wins	
7:00		
8:00		
9:00		
10:00		
11:00	Health and nutrition	
12:00		
13:00		
14:00	Today, I am grateful for...	
15:00		
16:00		
17:00	Today's self care	
18:00		
19:00		
20:00	Chart your cycle	
21:00		
22:00		
23:00	Positive affirmation	
Notes		

Thursday | 19 June 2025 - Waning Crescent

6:00		Today's quick wins
7:00		
8:00		
9:00		
10:00		
11:00		Health and nutrition
12:00		
13:00		
14:00		Today, I am grateful for...
15:00		
16:00		
17:00		Today's self care
18:00		
19:00		
20:00		Chart your cycle
21:00		
22:00		
23:00		Positive affirmation
Notes		

Friday | 20 June 2025 - Waning Crescent

6:00		Today's quick wins	
7:00			
8:00			
9:00			
10:00			
11:00		Health and nutrition	
12:00			
13:00			
14:00		Today, I am grateful for…	
15:00			
16:00			
17:00		Today's self care	
18:00			
19:00			
20:00		Chart your cycle	
21:00			
22:00			
23:00		Positive affirmation	
Notes			

Saturday | 21 June 2025 - Waning Crescent
Summer Solstice

6:00		Today's quick wins	
7:00			
8:00			
9:00			
10:00			
11:00		Health and nutrition	
12:00			
13:00			
14:00		Today, I am grateful for...	
15:00			
16:00			
17:00		Today's self care	
18:00			
19:00			
20:00		Chart your cycle	
21:00			
22:00			
23:00		Positive affirmation	
Notes			

Sunday | 22 June 2025 - Waning Crescent

6:00	Today's quick wins	
7:00		
8:00		
9:00		
10:00		
11:00	Health and nutrition	
12:00		
13:00		
14:00	Today, I am grateful for…	
15:00		
16:00		
17:00	Today's self care	
18:00		
19:00		
20:00	Chart your cycle	
21:00		
22:00		
23:00	Positive affirmation	
Notes		

Monday | 23 June 2025 - Waning Crescent

6:00		Today's quick wins	
7:00			
8:00			
9:00			
10:00			
11:00		Health and nutrition	
12:00			
13:00			
14:00		Today, I am grateful for...	
15:00			
16:00			
17:00		Today's self care	
18:00			
19:00			
20:00		Chart your cycle	
21:00			
22:00			
23:00		Positive affirmation	
Notes			

Tuesday | 24 June 2025 - Waning Crescent

6:00	**Today's quick wins**
7:00	
8:00	
9:00	
10:00	
11:00	**Health and nutrition**
12:00	
13:00	
14:00	**Today, I am grateful for...**
15:00	
16:00	
17:00	**Today's self care**
18:00	
19:00	
20:00	**Chart your cycle**
21:00	
22:00	
23:00	**Positive affirmation**
Notes	

Wednesday | 25 June 2025 - New Moon in Cancer at 10.31 GMT

6:00		Today's quick wins	
7:00			
8:00			
9:00			
10:00			
11:00		Health and nutrition	
12:00			
13:00			
14:00		Today, I am grateful for...	
15:00			
16:00			
17:00		Today's self care	
18:00			
19:00			
20:00		Chart your cycle	
21:00			
22:00			
23:00		Positive affirmation	
Notes			

Thursday | 26 June 2025 - Waxing Crescent

6:00	**Today's quick wins**
7:00	
8:00	
9:00	
10:00	
11:00	**Health and nutrition**
12:00	
13:00	
14:00	**Today, I am grateful for…**
15:00	
16:00	
17:00	**Today's self care**
18:00	
19:00	
20:00	**Chart your cycle**
21:00	
22:00	
23:00	**Positive affirmation**
Notes	

Friday | 27 June 2025 - Waxing Crescent

6:00		Today's quick wins
7:00		
8:00		
9:00		
10:00		
11:00		Health and nutrition
12:00		
13:00		
14:00		Today, I am grateful for...
15:00		
16:00		
17:00		Today's self care
18:00		
19:00		
20:00		Chart your cycle
21:00		
22:00		
23:00		Positive affirmation
Notes		

Saturday | 28 June 2025 - Waxing Crescent

6:00	**Today's quick wins**	
7:00		
8:00		
9:00		
10:00		
11:00	**Health and nutrition**	
12:00		
13:00		
14:00	**Today, I am grateful for...**	
15:00		
16:00		
17:00	**Today's self care**	
18:00		
19:00		
20:00	**Chart your cycle**	
21:00		
22:00		
23:00	**Positive affirmation**	
Notes		

Sunday | 29 June 2025 - Waxing Crescent

6:00	Today's quick wins
7:00	
8:00	
9:00	
10:00	
11:00	Health and nutrition
12:00	
13:00	
14:00	Today, I am grateful for…
15:00	
16:00	
17:00	Today's self care
18:00	
19:00	
20:00	Chart your cycle
21:00	
22:00	
23:00	Positive affirmation
Notes	

Monday | 30 June 2025 - Waxing Crescent

6:00	Today's quick wins	
7:00		
8:00		
9:00		
10:00		
11:00	Health and nutrition	
12:00		
13:00		
14:00	Today, I am grateful for…	
15:00		
16:00		
17:00	Today's self care	
18:00		
19:00		
20:00	Chart your cycle	
21:00		
22:00		
23:00	Positive affirmation	
Notes		

June achievements

Be proud of yourself and all that you have achieved this month. Write down your wins, big and small. If you have not achieved everything that you set out to do, that's okay! We learn and grow through our mistakes and experiences. You can use this space to make notes about anything that you have learned.

'Live life as if everything is rigged in your favour'
—Rumi

July 2025

Notes	Monday	Tuesday	Wednesday
	30	1	2
	7	8	9
	14	15	16
	21	22	23
	28	29	30

Thursday	Friday	Saturday	Sunday
3	4	5	6
10 ○	11	12	13
17	18 ☾	19	20
24 ●	25	26	27
31	1	2	3

July
Goddess Amaterasu

AMATERASU

Japanese Sun Goddess

All emperors of Japan are said to descend from her.

She brings the sun and light to the world, whilst her brother Tsukiyomi no Mikato is god of the moon. Their genders are exceptions in world myths of the sun and moon.

Along with light Amaterasu brings order and purity. She is at the very heart of the Shinto religion.

She is worshipped today at one of Japan's holiest sites. Pilgrims flock in their thousands to the Grand Shrine of Ise.

Books: Shinto the Kami Way by Sokyo Ono
Song: Satori Sunset by A.T.P
Moon phase: Waning moon
Crystal: Clear Quartz

My Vision for July

Tuesday | 1 July 2025 - Waxing Crescent

6:00		Today's quick wins
7:00		
8:00		
9:00		
10:00		
11:00		Health and nutrition
12:00		
13:00		
14:00		Today, I am grateful for...
15:00		
16:00		
17:00		Today's self care
18:00		
19:00		
20:00		Chart your cycle
21:00		
22:00		
23:00		Positive affirmation
Notes		

Wednesday | 2 July 2025 - First Quarter

6:00	Today's quick wins	
7:00		
8:00		
9:00		
10:00		
11:00	Health and nutrition	
12:00		
13:00		
14:00	Today, I am grateful for...	
15:00		
16:00		
17:00	Today's self care	
18:00		
19:00		
20:00	Chart your cycle	
21:00		
22:00		
23:00	Positive affirmation	
Notes		

Thursday | 3 July 2025 - Waxing Gibbous

6:00		Today's quick wins	
7:00			
8:00			
9:00			
10:00			
11:00		Health and nutrition	
12:00			
13:00			
14:00		Today, I am grateful for...	
15:00			
16:00			
17:00		Today's self care	
18:00			
19:00			
20:00		Chart your cycle	
21:00			
22:00			
23:00		Positive affirmation	
Notes			

Friday | 4 July 2025 - Waxing Gibbous

6:00	**Today's quick wins**
7:00	
8:00	
9:00	
10:00	
11:00	**Health and nutrition**
12:00	
13:00	
14:00	**Today, I am grateful for...**
15:00	
16:00	
17:00	**Today's self care**
18:00	
19:00	
20:00	**Chart your cycle**
21:00	
22:00	
23:00	**Positive affirmation**
Notes	

Saturday | 5 July 2025 - Waxing Gibbous

6:00		Today's quick wins	
7:00			
8:00			
9:00			
10:00			
11:00		Health and nutrition	
12:00			
13:00			
14:00		Today, I am grateful for...	
15:00			
16:00			
17:00		Today's self care	
18:00			
19:00			
20:00		Chart your cycle	
21:00			
22:00			
23:00		Positive affirmation	
Notes			

Sunday | 6 July 2025 - Waxing Gibbous

6:00	**Today's quick wins**
7:00	
8:00	
9:00	
10:00	
11:00	**Health and nutrition**
12:00	
13:00	
14:00	**Today, I am grateful for...**
15:00	
16:00	
17:00	**Today's self care**
18:00	
19:00	
20:00	**Chart your cycle**
21:00	
22:00	
23:00	**Positive affirmation**
Notes	

Monday | 7 July 2025 - Waxing Gibbous

6:00		Today's quick wins	
7:00			
8:00			
9:00			
10:00			
11:00		Health and nutrition	
12:00			
13:00			
14:00		Today, I am grateful for...	
15:00			
16:00			
17:00		Today's self care	
18:00			
19:00			
20:00		Chart your cycle	
21:00			
22:00			
23:00		Positive affirmation	
Notes			

Tuesday | 8 July 2025 - Waxing Gibbous

6:00	Today's quick wins	
7:00		
8:00		
9:00		
10:00		
11:00	Health and nutrition	
12:00		
13:00		
14:00	Today, I am grateful for...	
15:00		
16:00		
17:00	Today's self care	
18:00		
19:00		
20:00	Chart your cycle	
21:00		
22:00		
23:00	Positive affirmation	
Notes		

Wednesday | 9 July 2025 - Waxing Gibbous

6:00		Today's quick wins	
7:00			
8:00			
9:00			
10:00			
11:00		Health and nutrition	
12:00			
13:00			
14:00		Today, I am grateful for…	
15:00			
16:00			
17:00		Today's self care	
18:00			
19:00			
20:00		Chart your cycle	
21:00			
22:00			
23:00		Positive affirmation	
Notes			

Thursday | 10 July 2025 - Full Moon in Capricorn 20:36 GMT

6:00	**Today's quick wins**
7:00	
8:00	
9:00	
10:00	
11:00	**Health and nutrition**
12:00	
13:00	
14:00	**Today, I am grateful for...**
15:00	
16:00	
17:00	**Today's self care**
18:00	
19:00	
20:00	**Chart your cycle**
21:00	
22:00	
23:00	**Positive affirmation**
Notes	

Friday | 11 July 2025 - Waning Gibbous

6:00		Today's quick wins
7:00		
8:00		
9:00		
10:00		
11:00		Health and nutrition
12:00		
13:00		
14:00		Today, I am grateful for...
15:00		
16:00		
17:00		Today's self care
18:00		
19:00		
20:00		Chart your cycle
21:00		
22:00		
23:00		Positive affirmation
Notes		

Saturday | 12 July 2025 - Waning Gibbous

6:00	**Today's quick wins**
7:00	
8:00	
9:00	
10:00	
11:00	**Health and nutrition**
12:00	
13:00	
14:00	**Today, I am grateful for...**
15:00	
16:00	
17:00	**Today's self care**
18:00	
19:00	
20:00	**Chart your cycle**
21:00	
22:00	
23:00	**Positive affirmation**
Notes	

Sunday | 13 July 2025 - Waning Gibbous

6:00		Today's quick wins
7:00		
8:00		
9:00		
10:00		
11:00		Health and nutrition
12:00		
13:00		
14:00		Today, I am grateful for…
15:00		
16:00		
17:00		Today's self care
18:00		
19:00		
20:00		Chart your cycle
21:00		
22:00		
23:00		Positive affirmation
Notes		

Monday | 14 July 2025 - Waning Gibbous

6:00		Today's quick wins
7:00		
8:00		
9:00		
10:00		
11:00		Health and nutrition
12:00		
13:00		
14:00		Today, I am grateful for...
15:00		
16:00		
17:00		Today's self care
18:00		
19:00		
20:00		Chart your cycle
21:00		
22:00		
23:00		Positive affirmation
Notes		

Tuesday | 15 July 2025 - Waning Gibbous

6:00		Today's quick wins	
7:00			
8:00			
9:00			
10:00			
11:00		Health and nutrition	
12:00			
13:00			
14:00		Today, I am grateful for…	
15:00			
16:00			
17:00		Today's self care	
18:00			
19:00			
20:00		Chart your cycle	
21:00			
22:00			
23:00		Positive affirmation	
Notes			

Wednesday | 16 July 2025 - Waning Gibbous

6:00		**Today's quick wins**	
7:00			
8:00			
9:00			
10:00			
11:00		**Health and nutrition**	
12:00			
13:00			
14:00		**Today, I am grateful for...**	
15:00			
16:00			
17:00		**Today's self care**	
18:00			
19:00			
20:00		**Chart your cycle**	
21:00			
22:00			
23:00		**Positive affirmation**	
Notes			

Thursday | 17 July 2025 - Last Quarter

6:00	Today's quick wins	
7:00		
8:00		
9:00		
10:00		
11:00	Health and nutrition	
12:00		
13:00		
14:00	Today, I am grateful for…	
15:00		
16:00		
17:00	Today's self care	
18:00		
19:00		
20:00	Chart your cycle	
21:00		
22:00		
23:00	Positive affirmation	
Notes		

Friday | 18 July 2025 - Last Quarter

6:00	Today's quick wins	
7:00		
8:00		
9:00		
10:00		
11:00	Health and nutrition	
12:00		
13:00		
14:00	Today, I am grateful for…	
15:00		
16:00		
17:00	Today's self care	
18:00		
19:00		
20:00	Chart your cycle	
21:00		
22:00		
23:00	Positive affirmation	
Notes		

Saturday | 19 July 2025 - Waning Crescent

6:00	Today's quick wins	
7:00		
8:00		
9:00		
10:00		
11:00	Health and nutrition	
12:00		
13:00		
14:00	Today, I am grateful for…	
15:00		
16:00		
17:00	Today's self care	
18:00		
19:00		
20:00	Chart your cycle	
21:00		
22:00		
23:00	Positive affirmation	
Notes		

# Sunday | 20 July 2025 - Waning Crescent

6:00		**Today's quick wins**	
7:00			
8:00			
9:00			
10:00			
11:00		**Health and nutrition**	
12:00			
13:00			
14:00		**Today, I am grateful for...**	
15:00			
16:00			
17:00		**Today's self care**	
18:00			
19:00			
20:00		**Chart your cycle**	
21:00			
22:00			
23:00		**Positive affirmation**	
Notes			

Monday | 21 July 2025 - Waning Crescent

6:00		Today's quick wins
7:00		
8:00		
9:00		
10:00		
11:00		Health and nutrition
12:00		
13:00		
14:00		Today, I am grateful for...
15:00		
16:00		
17:00		Today's self care
18:00		
19:00		
20:00		Chart your cycle
21:00		
22:00		
23:00		Positive affirmation
Notes		

Tuesday | 22 July 2025 - Waning Crescent

6:00		Today's quick wins
7:00		
8:00		
9:00		
10:00		
11:00		Health and nutrition
12:00		
13:00		
14:00		Today, I am grateful for...
15:00		
16:00		
17:00		Today's self care
18:00		
19:00		
20:00		Chart your cycle
21:00		
22:00		
23:00		Positive affirmation
Notes		

Wednesday | 23 July 2025 - Waning Crescent

6:00		Today's quick wins	
7:00			
8:00			
9:00			
10:00			
11:00		Health and nutrition	
12:00			
13:00			
14:00		Today, I am grateful for...	
15:00			
16:00			
17:00		Today's self care	
18:00			
19:00			
20:00		Chart your cycle	
21:00			
22:00			
23:00		Positive affirmation	
Notes			

Thursday | 24 July 2025 - New Moon in Leo 19:10 GMT

6:00		Today's quick wins
7:00		
8:00		
9:00		
10:00		
11:00		Health and nutrition
12:00		
13:00		
14:00		Today, I am grateful for...
15:00		
16:00		
17:00		Today's self care
18:00		
19:00		
20:00		Chart your cycle
21:00		
22:00		
23:00		Positive affirmation
Notes		

Friday | 25 July 2025 - Waxing Crescent

6:00		Today's quick wins	
7:00			
8:00			
9:00			
10:00			
11:00		Health and nutrition	
12:00			
13:00			
14:00		Today, I am grateful for...	
15:00			
16:00			
17:00		Today's self care	
18:00			
19:00			
20:00		Chart your cycle	
21:00			
22:00			
23:00		Positive affirmation	
Notes			

Saturday | 26 July 2025 - Waxing Crescent

6:00	**Today's quick wins**
7:00	
8:00	
9:00	
10:00	
11:00	**Health and nutrition**
12:00	
13:00	
14:00	**Today, I am grateful for...**
15:00	
16:00	
17:00	**Today's self care**
18:00	
19:00	
20:00	**Chart your cycle**
21:00	
22:00	
23:00	**Positive affirmation**
Notes	

Sunday | 27 July 2025 - Waxing Crescent

6:00	Today's quick wins
7:00	
8:00	
9:00	
10:00	
11:00	Health and nutrition
12:00	
13:00	
14:00	Today, I am grateful for...
15:00	
16:00	
17:00	Today's self care
18:00	
19:00	
20:00	Chart your cycle
21:00	
22:00	
23:00	Positive affirmation
Notes	

Monday | 28 July 2025 - Waxing Crescent

6:00		Today's quick wins
7:00		
8:00		
9:00		
10:00		
11:00		Health and nutrition
12:00		
13:00		
14:00		Today, I am grateful for...
15:00		
16:00		
17:00		Today's self care
18:00		
19:00		
20:00		Chart your cycle
21:00		
22:00		
23:00		Positive affirmation
Notes		

Tuesday | 29 July 2025 - Waxing Crescent

6:00	Today's quick wins	
7:00		
8:00		
9:00		
10:00		
11:00	Health and nutrition	
12:00		
13:00		
14:00	Today, I am grateful for...	
15:00		
16:00		
17:00	Today's self care	
18:00		
19:00		
20:00	Chart your cycle	
21:00		
22:00		
23:00	Positive affirmation	
Notes		

Wednesday | 30 July 2025 - Waxing Crescent

6:00		Today's quick wins	
7:00			
8:00			
9:00			
10:00			
11:00		Health and nutrition	
12:00			
13:00			
14:00		Today, I am grateful for…	
15:00			
16:00			
17:00		Today's self care	
18:00			
19:00			
20:00		Chart your cycle	
21:00			
22:00			
23:00		Positive affirmation	
Notes			

Thursday | 31 July 2025 - Waxing Crescent

6:00	Today's quick wins	
7:00		
8:00		
9:00		
10:00		
11:00	Health and nutrition	
12:00		
13:00		
14:00	Today, I am grateful for…	
15:00		
16:00		
17:00	Today's self care	
18:00		
19:00		
20:00	Chart your cycle	
21:00		
22:00		
23:00	Positive affirmation	
Notes		

July achievements

Be proud of yourself and all that you have achieved this month. Write down your wins, big and small. If you have not achieved everything that you set out to do, that's okay! We learn and grow through our mistakes and experiences. You can use this space to make notes about anything that you have learned.

August 2025

Notes	Monday	Tuesday	Wednesday
	28	29	30
	4	5	6
	11	12	13
	18	19	20
	25	26	27

Thursday	Friday	Saturday	Sunday
31	1 ☾	2	3
7	8	9 ○	10
14	15	16 ☽	17
21	22	23 ●	24
28	29	30	31 ☾

August
Goddess Sif

SIF

Norse Goddess of Grain and Fertility.

A giantess with golden blonde hair.

The etymology of her name relates to family and connections. Residents of rural farming areas in Sweden referred to Sif as Godmother.

Her beginnings are unknown. Ancient texts never refer to her parents, we know only that she was the second wife of Norse God Thor. Together they made a powerful couple, he is the god of weather and sky whilst she is an earth goddess symbolising fertility and harvest.

Books: Norse Myths by Matt Ralphs
Song: Sweet Earth by Carrie Tree
Moon phase: Waxing moon
Crystal: Malachite

My Vision for August

Friday | 1 August 2025 - First Quarter

6:00		Today's quick wins
7:00		
8:00		
9:00		
10:00		
11:00		Health and nutrition
12:00		
13:00		
14:00		Today, I am grateful for...
15:00		
16:00		
17:00		Today's self care
18:00		
19:00		
20:00		Chart your cycle
21:00		
22:00		
23:00		Positive affirmation
Notes		

Saturday | 2 August 2025 - Waxing Gibbous

6:00	**Today's quick wins**
7:00	
8:00	
9:00	
10:00	
11:00	**Health and nutrition**
12:00	
13:00	
14:00	**Today, I am grateful for...**
15:00	
16:00	
17:00	**Today's self care**
18:00	
19:00	
20:00	**Chart your cycle**
21:00	
22:00	
23:00	**Positive affirmation**
Notes	

Sunday | 3 August 2025 - Waxing Gibbous

6:00		Today's quick wins	
7:00			
8:00			
9:00			
10:00			
11:00		Health and nutrition	
12:00			
13:00			
14:00		Today, I am grateful for…	
15:00			
16:00			
17:00		Today's self care	
18:00			
19:00			
20:00		Chart your cycle	
21:00			
22:00			
23:00		Positive affirmation	
Notes			

Monday | 4 August 2025 - Waxing Gibbous

6:00	Today's quick wins	
7:00		
8:00		
9:00		
10:00		
11:00	Health and nutrition	
12:00		
13:00		
14:00	Today, I am grateful for...	
15:00		
16:00		
17:00	Today's self care	
18:00		
19:00		
20:00	Chart your cycle	
21:00		
22:00		
23:00	Positive affirmation	
Notes		

Tuesday | 5 August 2025 - Waxing Gibbous

6:00	Today's quick wins	
7:00		
8:00		
9:00		
10:00		
11:00	Health and nutrition	
12:00		
13:00		
14:00	Today, I am grateful for...	
15:00		
16:00		
17:00	Today's self care	
18:00		
19:00		
20:00	Chart your cycle	
21:00		
22:00		
23:00	Positive affirmation	
Notes		

Wednesday | 6 August 2025 - Waxing Gibbous

6:00		Today's quick wins
7:00		
8:00		
9:00		
10:00		
11:00		Health and nutrition
12:00		
13:00		
14:00		Today, I am grateful for...
15:00		
16:00		
17:00		Today's self care
18:00		
19:00		
20:00		Chart your cycle
21:00		
22:00		
23:00		Positive affirmation
Notes		

Thursday | 7 August 2025 - Waxing Gibbous

6:00	**Today's quick wins**
7:00	
8:00	
9:00	
10:00	
11:00	**Health and nutrition**
12:00	
13:00	
14:00	**Today, I am grateful for...**
15:00	
16:00	
17:00	**Today's self care**
18:00	
19:00	
20:00	**Chart your cycle**
21:00	
22:00	
23:00	**Positive affirmation**
Notes	

Friday | 8 August 2025 - Waxing Gibbous

6:00	Today's quick wins	
7:00		
8:00		
9:00		
10:00		
11:00	Health and nutrition	
12:00		
13:00		
14:00	Today, I am grateful for…	
15:00		
16:00		
17:00	Today's self care	
18:00		
19:00		
20:00	Chart your cycle	
21:00		
22:00		
23:00	Positive affirmation	
Notes		

Saturday | 9 August 2025 - Full Moon in Aquarius 07:54 GMT

6:00	Today's quick wins	
7:00		
8:00		
9:00		
10:00		
11:00	Health and nutrition	
12:00		
13:00		
14:00	Today, I am grateful for…	
15:00		
16:00		
17:00	Today's self care	
18:00		
19:00		
20:00	Chart your cycle	
21:00		
22:00		
23:00	Positive affirmation	
Notes		

Sunday | 10 August 2025 - Waning Gibbous

6:00	**Today's quick wins**
7:00	
8:00	
9:00	
10:00	
11:00	**Health and nutrition**
12:00	
13:00	
14:00	**Today, I am grateful for...**
15:00	
16:00	
17:00	**Today's self care**
18:00	
19:00	
20:00	**Chart your cycle**
21:00	
22:00	
23:00	**Positive affirmation**
Notes	

Monday | 11 August 2025 - Waning Gibbous

6:00	Today's quick wins
7:00	
8:00	
9:00	
10:00	
11:00	Health and nutrition
12:00	
13:00	
14:00	Today, I am grateful for...
15:00	
16:00	
17:00	Today's self care
18:00	
19:00	
20:00	Chart your cycle
21:00	
22:00	
23:00	Positive affirmation
Notes	

Tuesday | 12 August 2025 - Waning Gibbous

6:00	**Today's quick wins**
7:00	
8:00	
9:00	
10:00	
11:00	**Health and nutrition**
12:00	
13:00	
14:00	**Today, I am grateful for...**
15:00	
16:00	
17:00	**Today's self care**
18:00	
19:00	
20:00	**Chart your cycle**
21:00	
22:00	
23:00	**Positive affirmation**
Notes	

Wednesday | 13 August 2025 - Waning Gibbous

6:00	Today's quick wins
7:00	
8:00	
9:00	
10:00	
11:00	Health and nutrition
12:00	
13:00	
14:00	Today, I am grateful for...
15:00	
16:00	
17:00	Today's self care
18:00	
19:00	
20:00	Chart your cycle
21:00	
22:00	
23:00	Positive affirmation
Notes	

Thursday | 14 August 2025 - Waning Gibbous

6:00	Today's quick wins
7:00	
8:00	
9:00	
10:00	
11:00	Health and nutrition
12:00	
13:00	
14:00	Today, I am grateful for...
15:00	
16:00	
17:00	Today's self care
18:00	
19:00	
20:00	Chart your cycle
21:00	
22:00	
23:00	Positive affirmation
Notes	

Friday | 15 August 2025 - Waning Gibbous

6:00		Today's quick wins	
7:00			
8:00			
9:00			
10:00			
11:00		Health and nutrition	
12:00			
13:00			
14:00		Today, I am grateful for...	
15:00			
16:00			
17:00		Today's self care	
18:00			
19:00			
20:00		Chart your cycle	
21:00			
22:00			
23:00		Positive affirmation	
Notes			

Saturday | 16 August 2025 - Last Quarter

6:00	**Today's quick wins**
7:00	
8:00	
9:00	
10:00	
11:00	**Health and nutrition**
12:00	
13:00	
14:00	**Today, I am grateful for...**
15:00	
16:00	
17:00	**Today's self care**
18:00	
19:00	
20:00	**Chart your cycle**
21:00	
22:00	
23:00	**Positive affirmation**
Notes	

Sunday | 17 August 2025 - Waning Crescent

6:00	Today's quick wins	
7:00		
8:00		
9:00		
10:00		
11:00	Health and nutrition	
12:00		
13:00		
14:00	Today, I am grateful for...	
15:00		
16:00		
17:00	Today's self care	
18:00		
19:00		
20:00	Chart your cycle	
21:00		
22:00		
23:00	Positive affirmation	
Notes		

Monday | 18 August 2025 - Waning Crescent

6:00	**Today's quick wins**
7:00	
8:00	
9:00	
10:00	
11:00	**Health and nutrition**
12:00	
13:00	
14:00	**Today, I am grateful for...**
15:00	
16:00	
17:00	**Today's self care**
18:00	
19:00	
20:00	**Chart your cycle**
21:00	
22:00	
23:00	**Positive affirmation**
Notes	

Tuesday | 19 August 2025 - Waning Crescent

6:00		Today's quick wins
7:00		
8:00		
9:00		
10:00		
11:00		Health and nutrition
12:00		
13:00		
14:00		Today, I am grateful for...
15:00		
16:00		
17:00		Today's self care
18:00		
19:00		
20:00		Chart your cycle
21:00		
22:00		
23:00		Positive affirmation
Notes		

Wednesday | 20 August 2025 - Waning Crescent

6:00		Today's quick wins	
7:00			
8:00			
9:00			
10:00			
11:00		Health and nutrition	
12:00			
13:00			
14:00		Today, I am grateful for…	
15:00			
16:00			
17:00		Today's self care	
18:00			
19:00			
20:00		Chart your cycle	
21:00			
22:00			
23:00		Positive affirmation	
Notes			

Thursday | 21 August 2025 - Waning Crescent

6:00		Today's quick wins	
7:00			
8:00			
9:00			
10:00			
11:00		Health and nutrition	
12:00			
13:00			
14:00		Today, I am grateful for...	
15:00			
16:00			
17:00		Today's self care	
18:00			
19:00			
20:00		Chart your cycle	
21:00			
22:00			
23:00		Positive affirmation	
Notes			

Friday | 22 August 2025 - Waning Crescent

6:00	Today's quick wins
7:00	
8:00	
9:00	
10:00	
11:00	Health and nutrition
12:00	
13:00	
14:00	Today, I am grateful for...
15:00	
16:00	
17:00	Today's self care
18:00	
19:00	
20:00	Chart your cycle
21:00	
22:00	
23:00	Positive affirmation
Notes	

Saturday | 23 August 2025 - New Moon in Virgo 06:06 GMT

6:00	Today's quick wins
7:00	
8:00	
9:00	
10:00	
11:00	Health and nutrition
12:00	
13:00	
14:00	Today, I am grateful for...
15:00	
16:00	
17:00	Today's self care
18:00	
19:00	
20:00	Chart your cycle
21:00	
22:00	
23:00	Positive affirmation
Notes	

Sunday | 24 August 2025 - Waxing Crescent

6:00	**Today's quick wins**
7:00	
8:00	
9:00	
10:00	
11:00	**Health and nutrition**
12:00	
13:00	
14:00	**Today, I am grateful for…**
15:00	
16:00	
17:00	**Today's self care**
18:00	
19:00	
20:00	**Chart your cycle**
21:00	
22:00	
23:00	**Positive affirmation**
Notes	

Monday | 25 August 2025 - Waxing Crescent

6:00	Today's quick wins	
7:00		
8:00		
9:00		
10:00		
11:00	Health and nutrition	
12:00		
13:00		
14:00	Today, I am grateful for...	
15:00		
16:00		
17:00	Today's self care	
18:00		
19:00		
20:00	Chart your cycle	
21:00		
22:00		
23:00	Positive affirmation	
Notes		

Tuesday | 26 August 2025 - Waxing Crescent

6:00	**Today's quick wins**
7:00	
8:00	
9:00	
10:00	
11:00	**Health and nutrition**
12:00	
13:00	
14:00	**Today, I am grateful for...**
15:00	
16:00	
17:00	**Today's self care**
18:00	
19:00	
20:00	**Chart your cycle**
21:00	
22:00	
23:00	**Positive affirmation**
Notes	

Wednesday | 27 August 2025 - Waxing Crescent

6:00	Today's quick wins	
7:00		
8:00		
9:00		
10:00		
11:00	Health and nutrition	
12:00		
13:00		
14:00	Today, I am grateful for…	
15:00		
16:00		
17:00	Today's self care	
18:00		
19:00		
20:00	Chart your cycle	
21:00		
22:00		
23:00	Positive affirmation	
Notes		

Thursday | 28 August 2025 - Waxing Crescent

6:00		Today's quick wins	
7:00			
8:00			
9:00			
10:00			
11:00		Health and nutrition	
12:00			
13:00			
14:00		Today, I am grateful for...	
15:00			
16:00			
17:00		Today's self care	
18:00			
19:00			
20:00		Chart your cycle	
21:00			
22:00			
23:00		Positive affirmation	
Notes			

Friday | 29 August 2025 - Waxing Crescent

6:00	Today's quick wins	
7:00		
8:00		
9:00		
10:00		
11:00	Health and nutrition	
12:00		
13:00		
14:00	Today, I am grateful for...	
15:00		
16:00		
17:00	Today's self care	
18:00		
19:00		
20:00	Chart your cycle	
21:00		
22:00		
23:00	Positive affirmation	
Notes		

Saturday | 30 August 2025 - Waxing Crescent

6:00	**Today's quick wins**
7:00	
8:00	
9:00	
10:00	
11:00	**Health and nutrition**
12:00	
13:00	
14:00	**Today, I am grateful for…**
15:00	
16:00	
17:00	**Today's self care**
18:00	
19:00	
20:00	**Chart your cycle**
21:00	
22:00	
23:00	**Positive affirmation**
Notes	

# Sunday | 31 August 2025 - First Quarter

6:00	Today's quick wins	
7:00		
8:00		
9:00		
10:00		
11:00	Health and nutrition	
12:00		
13:00		
14:00	Today, I am grateful for…	
15:00		
16:00		
17:00	Today's self care	
18:00		
19:00		
20:00	Chart your cycle	
21:00		
22:00		
23:00	Positive affirmation	
Notes		

August achievements

Be proud of yourself and all that you have achieved this month. Write down your wins, big and small. If you have not achieved everything that you set out to do, that's okay! We learn and grow through our mistakes and experiences. You can use this space to make notes about anything that you have learned.

September 2025

Notes	Monday	Tuesday	Wednesday
	1	2	3
	8	9	10
	15	16	17
	22 *Autumn Equinox*	23	24
	29	30	

Thursday	Friday	Saturday	Sunday
4	5	6	7 ○
11	12	13	14 ☽
18	19	20	21 ●
25	26	27	28
2	3	4	5

September
Mary Magdalene

MARY MAGDALENE

'The Rose'

Left out of the original canon, and rediscovered in Egypt in 1896 (with half of its pages missing) the Gospel of Mary Magdalene reveals the deeper, truer meaning of Christianity's metaphysical origins. It tells us that God is not out there separate from us, but within each of us. Gnostic Gospels claim that *Jesus loved Mary Magdalene most of all and he kissed her on the mouth.*
Pope Gregory I turned her into a prostitute.
Was she Jesus' wife? Did they have children? We may never know for sure, but she was seemingly a threat to the church - and the origins of Christianity were purposefully altered along the way.
If we learn anything from Mary it is to keep an open mind, do our research and listen to our hearts.
Sometimes the truth is hidden.

Book: Mary Magdalene, the Way of the Rose by Ishtara Ammuna Rose
Song: Rose Lineage by Marya Stark, Mama Crow and Benjy Weatheimer
Crystal: Rhodonite
Moon phase: Full Moon

My Vision for September

Monday | 1 September 2025 - Waxing Gibbous

6:00	Today's quick wins	
7:00		
8:00		
9:00		
10:00		
11:00	Health and nutrition	
12:00		
13:00		
14:00	Today, I am grateful for…	
15:00		
16:00		
17:00	Today's self care	
18:00		
19:00		
20:00	Chart your cycle	
21:00		
22:00		
23:00	Positive affirmation	
Notes		

Tuesday | 2 September 2025 - Waxing Gibbous

6:00	**Today's quick wins**	
7:00		
8:00		
9:00		
10:00		
11:00	**Health and nutrition**	
12:00		
13:00		
14:00	**Today, I am grateful for...**	
15:00		
16:00		
17:00	**Today's self care**	
18:00		
19:00		
20:00	**Chart your cycle**	
21:00		
22:00		
23:00	**Positive affirmation**	
Notes		

Wednesday | 3 September 2025 - Waxing Gibbous

6:00		Today's quick wins	
7:00			
8:00			
9:00			
10:00			
11:00		Health and nutrition	
12:00			
13:00			
14:00		Today, I am grateful for…	
15:00			
16:00			
17:00		Today's self care	
18:00			
19:00			
20:00		Chart your cycle	
21:00			
22:00			
23:00		Positive affirmation	
Notes			

Thursday | 4 September 2025 - Waxing Gibbous

Time		Section	
6:00		**Today's quick wins**	
7:00			
8:00			
9:00			
10:00			
11:00		**Health and nutrition**	
12:00			
13:00			
14:00		**Today, I am grateful for…**	
15:00			
16:00			
17:00		**Today's self care**	
18:00			
19:00			
20:00		**Chart your cycle**	
21:00			
22:00			
23:00		**Positive affirmation**	

Notes

Friday | 5 September 2025 - Waxing Gibbous

Time		Section	
6:00		Today's quick wins	
7:00			
8:00			
9:00			
10:00			
11:00		Health and nutrition	
12:00			
13:00			
14:00		Today, I am grateful for...	
15:00			
16:00			
17:00		Today's self care	
18:00			
19:00			
20:00		Chart your cycle	
21:00			
22:00			
23:00		Positive affirmation	
Notes			

Saturday | 6 September 2025 - Waxing Gibbous

6:00	**Today's quick wins**
7:00	
8:00	
9:00	
10:00	
11:00	**Health and nutrition**
12:00	
13:00	
14:00	**Today, I am grateful for…**
15:00	
16:00	
17:00	**Today's self care**
18:00	
19:00	
20:00	**Chart your cycle**
21:00	
22:00	
23:00	**Positive affirmation**
Notes	

Sunday | 7 September 2025 - Full Moon Lunar Eclipse In Pisces
18:08 GMT

6:00		Today's quick wins
7:00		
8:00		
9:00		
10:00		
11:00		Health and nutrition
12:00		
13:00		
14:00		Today, I am grateful for...
15:00		
16:00		
17:00		Today's self care
18:00		
19:00		
20:00		Chart your cycle
21:00		
22:00		
23:00		Positive affirmation
Notes		

Monday | 8 September 2025 - Waning Gibbous

6:00	**Today's quick wins**
7:00	
8:00	
9:00	
10:00	
11:00	**Health and nutrition**
12:00	
13:00	
14:00	**Today, I am grateful for...**
15:00	
16:00	
17:00	**Today's self care**
18:00	
19:00	
20:00	**Chart your cycle**
21:00	
22:00	
23:00	**Positive affirmation**
Notes	

Tuesday | 9 September 2025 - Waning Gibbous

6:00	Today's quick wins
7:00	
8:00	
9:00	
10:00	
11:00	Health and nutrition
12:00	
13:00	
14:00	Today, I am grateful for…
15:00	
16:00	
17:00	Today's self care
18:00	
19:00	
20:00	Chart your cycle
21:00	
22:00	
23:00	Positive affirmation
Notes	

Wednesday | 10 September - Waning Gibbous

Time		Section	
6:00		Today's quick wins	
7:00			
8:00			
9:00			
10:00			
11:00		Health and nutrition	
12:00			
13:00			
14:00		Today, I am grateful for…	
15:00			
16:00			
17:00		Today's self care	
18:00			
19:00			
20:00		Chart your cycle	
21:00			
22:00			
23:00		Positive affirmation	
Notes			

Thursday | 11 September 2025 - Waning Gibbous

6:00	Today's quick wins	
7:00		
8:00		
9:00		
10:00		
11:00	Health and nutrition	
12:00		
13:00		
14:00	Today, I am grateful for…	
15:00		
16:00		
17:00	Today's self care	
18:00		
19:00		
20:00	Chart your cycle	
21:00		
22:00		
23:00	Positive affirmation	
Notes		

Friday | 12 September 2025 - Waning Gibbous

6:00	Today's quick wins	
7:00		
8:00		
9:00		
10:00		
11:00	Health and nutrition	
12:00		
13:00		
14:00	Today, I am grateful for...	
15:00		
16:00		
17:00	Today's self care	
18:00		
19:00		
20:00	Chart your cycle	
21:00		
22:00		
23:00	Positive affirmation	
Notes		

Saturday | 13 September 2025 - Waning Gibbous

6:00	**Today's quick wins**
7:00	
8:00	
9:00	
10:00	
11:00	**Health and nutrition**
12:00	
13:00	
14:00	**Today, I am grateful for...**
15:00	
16:00	
17:00	**Today's self care**
18:00	
19:00	
20:00	**Chart your cycle**
21:00	
22:00	
23:00	**Positive affirmation**
Notes	

Sunday | 14 September 2025 - Last Quarter

6:00	**Today's quick wins**
7:00	
8:00	
9:00	
10:00	
11:00	**Health and nutrition**
12:00	
13:00	
14:00	**Today, I am grateful for...**
15:00	
16:00	
17:00	**Today's self care**
18:00	
19:00	
20:00	**Chart your cycle**
21:00	
22:00	
23:00	**Positive affirmation**
Notes	

Monday | 15 September 2025 - Waning Crescent

6:00	Today's quick wins
7:00	
8:00	
9:00	
10:00	
11:00	Health and nutrition
12:00	
13:00	
14:00	Today, I am grateful for...
15:00	
16:00	
17:00	Today's self care
18:00	
19:00	
20:00	Chart your cycle
21:00	
22:00	
23:00	Positive affirmation
Notes	

Tuesday | 16 September 2025 - Waning Crescent

Time		Section	
6:00		Today's quick wins	
7:00			
8:00			
9:00			
10:00			
11:00		Health and nutrition	
12:00			
13:00			
14:00		Today, I am grateful for...	
15:00			
16:00			
17:00		Today's self care	
18:00			
19:00			
20:00		Chart your cycle	
21:00			
22:00			
23:00		Positive affirmation	
Notes			

Wednesday | 17 September 2025 - Waning Crescent

6:00	Today's quick wins	
7:00		
8:00		
9:00		
10:00		
11:00	Health and nutrition	
12:00		
13:00		
14:00	Today, I am grateful for…	
15:00		
16:00		
17:00	Today's self care	
18:00		
19:00		
20:00	Chart your cycle	
21:00		
22:00		
23:00	Positive affirmation	
Notes		

Thursday | 18 September 2025 - **Waning Crescent**

6:00	**Today's quick wins**
7:00	
8:00	
9:00	
10:00	
11:00	**Health and nutrition**
12:00	
13:00	
14:00	**Today, I am grateful for...**
15:00	
16:00	
17:00	**Today's self care**
18:00	
19:00	
20:00	**Chart your cycle**
21:00	
22:00	
23:00	**Positive affirmation**
Notes	

Friday | 19 September 2025 - Waning Crescent

6:00		Today's quick wins
7:00		
8:00		
9:00		
10:00		
11:00		Health and nutrition
12:00		
13:00		
14:00		Today, I am grateful for...
15:00		
16:00		
17:00		Today's self care
18:00		
19:00		
20:00		Chart your cycle
21:00		
22:00		
23:00		Positive affirmation
Notes		

Saturday | 20 September 2025 - Waning Crescent

6:00		Today's quick wins
7:00		
8:00		
9:00		
10:00		
11:00		Health and nutrition
12:00		
13:00		
14:00		Today, I am grateful for...
15:00		
16:00		
17:00		Today's self care
18:00		
19:00		
20:00		Chart your cycle
21:00		
22:00		
23:00		Positive affirmation
Notes		

Sunday | 21 September 2025 - New Moon Solar Eclipse in Virgo 19:53 GMT into Libra at 21.41

6:00		Today's quick wins
7:00		
8:00		
9:00		
10:00		
11:00		Health and nutrition
12:00		
13:00		
14:00		Today, I am grateful for…
15:00		
16:00		
17:00		Today's self care
18:00		
19:00		
20:00		Chart your cycle
21:00		
22:00		
23:00		Positive affirmation
Notes		

Monday | 22 September 2025 - Waxing Crescent

6:00	**Today's quick wins**
7:00	
8:00	
9:00	
10:00	
11:00	**Health and nutrition**
12:00	
13:00	
14:00	**Today, I am grateful for...**
15:00	
16:00	
17:00	**Today's self care**
18:00	
19:00	
20:00	**Chart your cycle**
21:00	
22:00	
23:00	**Positive affirmation**
Notes	

Tuesday | 23 September 2025 - Waxing Crescent

6:00	Today's quick wins
7:00	
8:00	
9:00	
10:00	
11:00	Health and nutrition
12:00	
13:00	
14:00	Today, I am grateful for...
15:00	
16:00	
17:00	Today's self care
18:00	
19:00	
20:00	Chart your cycle
21:00	
22:00	
23:00	Positive affirmation
Notes	

Wednesday | 24 September 2025 - Waxing Crescent

6:00		Today's quick wins	
7:00			
8:00			
9:00			
10:00			
11:00		Health and nutrition	
12:00			
13:00			
14:00		Today, I am grateful for...	
15:00			
16:00			
17:00		Today's self care	
18:00			
19:00			
20:00		Chart your cycle	
21:00			
22:00			
23:00		Positive affirmation	
Notes			

Thursday | 25 September - Waxing Crescent

6:00	**Today's quick wins**
7:00	
8:00	
9:00	
10:00	
11:00	**Health and nutrition**
12:00	
13:00	
14:00	**Today, I am grateful for...**
15:00	
16:00	
17:00	**Today's self care**
18:00	
19:00	
20:00	**Chart your cycle**
21:00	
22:00	
23:00	**Positive affirmation**
Notes	

Friday | 26 September 2025 - Waxing Crescent

6:00	Today's quick wins	
7:00		
8:00		
9:00		
10:00		
11:00	Health and nutrition	
12:00		
13:00		
14:00	Today, I am grateful for...	
15:00		
16:00		
17:00	Today's self care	
18:00		
19:00		
20:00	Chart your cycle	
21:00		
22:00		
23:00	Positive affirmation	
Notes		

Saturday | 27 September 2025 - Waxing Crescent

6:00	Today's quick wins	
7:00		
8:00		
9:00		
10:00		
11:00	Health and nutrition	
12:00		
13:00		
14:00	Today, I am grateful for...	
15:00		
16:00		
17:00	Today's self care	
18:00		
19:00		
20:00	Chart your cycle	
21:00		
22:00		
23:00	Positive affirmation	
Notes		

Sunday | 28 September 2025 - Waxing Crescent

6:00	**Today's quick wins**
7:00	
8:00	
9:00	
10:00	
11:00	**Health and nutrition**
12:00	
13:00	
14:00	**Today, I am grateful for...**
15:00	
16:00	
17:00	**Today's self care**
18:00	
19:00	
20:00	**Chart your cycle**
21:00	
22:00	
23:00	**Positive affirmation**
Notes	

Monday | 29 September 2025 - First Quarter

6:00	Today's quick wins	
7:00		
8:00		
9:00		
10:00		
11:00	Health and nutrition	
12:00		
13:00		
14:00	Today, I am grateful for…	
15:00		
16:00		
17:00	Today's self care	
18:00		
19:00		
20:00	Chart your cycle	
21:00		
22:00		
23:00	Positive affirmation	
Notes		

Tuesday | 30 September 2025 - First Quarter

6:00		Today's quick wins	
7:00			
8:00			
9:00			
10:00			
11:00		Health and nutrition	
12:00			
13:00			
14:00		Today, I am grateful for...	
15:00			
16:00			
17:00		Today's self care	
18:00			
19:00			
20:00		Chart your cycle	
21:00			
22:00			
23:00		Positive affirmation	
Notes			

September achievements

Be proud of yourself and all that you have achieved this month. Write down your wins, big and small. If you have not achieved everything that you set out to do, that's okay! We learn and grow through our mistakes and experiences. You can use this space to make notes about anything that you have learned.

'If you follow your heart, if you listen to your gut, and if you extend your hand to help another — not for any agenda, but for the sake of humanity — you are going to find the truth.'

— Erin Brockovich

October 2025

Notes	Monday	Tuesday	Wednesday
	29	30	1
	6	7	8
	13	14	15
	20	21	22
	27	28	29

Thursday	Friday	Saturday	Sunday
2	3	4	5
9	10	11	12
16	17	18	19
23	24	25	26
30	31		

October
Goddess Cerridwen

CERRIDWEN

Celtic Goddess of Inspiration and Rebirth.
Keeper of the cauldron of knowledge.

A white witch with a powerful gift of prophecy.

The potions concocted and brewed in her cauldron helped others. She had a divine knowledge of the cycle of life, birth, death and rebirth.

She understood the link between female cycles and the changing seasons.

Tuning into Cerridwen helps us to release what no longer serves and let it go. Especially powerful during the dark moon.

Books: Witch by Lisa Lister
Song: Burning Times by Elaine Silver
Moon phase: Dark moon
Crystal: Black Obsidian

My Vision for October

Wednesday | 1 October 2025 - Waxing Gibbous

6:00	Today's quick wins
7:00	
8:00	
9:00	
10:00	
11:00	Health and nutrition
12:00	
13:00	
14:00	Today, I am grateful for...
15:00	
16:00	
17:00	Today's self care
18:00	
19:00	
20:00	Chart your cycle
21:00	
22:00	
23:00	Positive affirmation
Notes	

Thursday | 2 October 2025 - Waxing Gibbous

6:00	Today's quick wins	
7:00		
8:00		
9:00		
10:00		
11:00	Health and nutrition	
12:00		
13:00		
14:00	Today, I am grateful for...	
15:00		
16:00		
17:00	Today's self care	
18:00		
19:00		
20:00	Chart your cycle	
21:00		
22:00		
23:00	Positive affirmation	
Notes		

Friday | 3 October 2025 - Waxing Gibbous

6:00		Today's quick wins	
7:00			
8:00			
9:00			
10:00			
11:00		Health and nutrition	
12:00			
13:00			
14:00		Today, I am grateful for...	
15:00			
16:00			
17:00		Today's self care	
18:00			
19:00			
20:00		Chart your cycle	
21:00			
22:00			
23:00		Positive affirmation	
Notes			

Saturday | 4 October 2025 - Waxing Gibbous

6:00	Today's quick wins	
7:00		
8:00		
9:00		
10:00		
11:00	Health and nutrition	
12:00		
13:00		
14:00	Today, I am grateful for...	
15:00		
16:00		
17:00	Today's self care	
18:00		
19:00		
20:00	Chart your cycle	
21:00		
22:00		
23:00	Positive affirmation	
Notes		

Sunday | 5 October 2025 - Waxing Gibbous

6:00	**Today's quick wins**
7:00	
8:00	
9:00	
10:00	
11:00	**Health and nutrition**
12:00	
13:00	
14:00	**Today, I am grateful for…**
15:00	
16:00	
17:00	**Today's self care**
18:00	
19:00	
20:00	**Chart your cycle**
21:00	
22:00	
23:00	**Positive affirmation**
Notes	

Monday | 6 October 2025 - Waxing Gibbous

6:00		Today's quick wins	
7:00			
8:00			
9:00			
10:00			
11:00		Health and nutrition	
12:00			
13:00			
14:00		Today, I am grateful for…	
15:00			
16:00			
17:00		Today's self care	
18:00			
19:00			
20:00		Chart your cycle	
21:00			
22:00			
23:00		Positive affirmation	
Notes			

Tuesday | 7 October 2025 - Full Moon in Aries 03:47 GMT

6:00		**Today's quick wins**	
7:00			
8:00			
9:00			
10:00			
11:00		**Health and nutrition**	
12:00			
13:00			
14:00		**Today, I am grateful for...**	
15:00			
16:00			
17:00		**Today's self care**	
18:00			
19:00			
20:00		**Chart your cycle**	
21:00			
22:00			
23:00		**Positive affirmation**	
Notes			

Wednesday | 8 October 2025 - Waning Gibbous

6:00		Today's quick wins	
7:00			
8:00			
9:00			
10:00			
11:00		Health and nutrition	
12:00			
13:00			
14:00		Today, I am grateful for...	
15:00			
16:00			
17:00		Today's self care	
18:00			
19:00			
20:00		Chart your cycle	
21:00			
22:00			
23:00		Positive affirmation	
Notes			

Thursday | 9 October 2025 - Waning Gibbous

6:00		Today's quick wins
7:00		
8:00		
9:00		
10:00		
11:00		Health and nutrition
12:00		
13:00		
14:00		Today, I am grateful for…
15:00		
16:00		
17:00		Today's self care
18:00		
19:00		
20:00		Chart your cycle
21:00		
22:00		
23:00		Positive affirmation
Notes		

Friday | 10 October 2025 - Waning Gibbous

6:00	**Today's quick wins**
7:00	
8:00	
9:00	
10:00	
11:00	**Health and nutrition**
12:00	
13:00	
14:00	**Today, I am grateful for...**
15:00	
16:00	
17:00	**Today's self care**
18:00	
19:00	
20:00	**Chart your cycle**
21:00	
22:00	
23:00	**Positive affirmation**
Notes	

Saturday | 11 October 2025 - Waning Gibbous

6:00	Today's quick wins
7:00	
8:00	
9:00	
10:00	
11:00	Health and nutrition
12:00	
13:00	
14:00	Today, I am grateful for...
15:00	
16:00	
17:00	Today's self care
18:00	
19:00	
20:00	Chart your cycle
21:00	
22:00	
23:00	Positive affirmation
Notes	

Sunday | 12 October 2025 - Waning Gibbous

6:00	**Today's quick wins**
7:00	
8:00	
9:00	
10:00	
11:00	**Health and nutrition**
12:00	
13:00	
14:00	**Today, I am grateful for...**
15:00	
16:00	
17:00	**Today's self care**
18:00	
19:00	
20:00	**Chart your cycle**
21:00	
22:00	
23:00	**Positive affirmation**
Notes	

Monday | 13 October 2025 - Last Quarter

6:00	Today's quick wins
7:00	
8:00	
9:00	
10:00	
11:00	Health and nutrition
12:00	
13:00	
14:00	Today, I am grateful for...
15:00	
16:00	
17:00	Today's self care
18:00	
19:00	
20:00	Chart your cycle
21:00	
22:00	
23:00	Positive affirmation
Notes	

Tuesday | 14 October 2025 - Waning Crescent

6:00	Today's quick wins	
7:00		
8:00		
9:00		
10:00		
11:00	Health and nutrition	
12:00		
13:00		
14:00	Today, I am grateful for...	
15:00		
16:00		
17:00	Today's self care	
18:00		
19:00		
20:00	Chart your cycle	
21:00		
22:00		
23:00	Positive affirmation	
Notes		

Wednesday | 15 October 2025 - Waning Crescent

6:00	
7:00	
8:00	
9:00	
10:00	
11:00	
12:00	
13:00	
14:00	
15:00	
16:00	
17:00	
18:00	
19:00	
20:00	
21:00	
22:00	
23:00	
Notes	

Today's quick wins

Health and nutrition

Today, I am grateful for…

Today's self care

Chart your cycle

Positive affirmation

Thursday | 16 October 2025 - Waning Crescent

6:00		Today's quick wins	
7:00			
8:00			
9:00			
10:00			
11:00		Health and nutrition	
12:00			
13:00			
14:00		Today, I am grateful for…	
15:00			
16:00			
17:00		Today's self care	
18:00			
19:00			
20:00		Chart your cycle	
21:00			
22:00			
23:00		Positive affirmation	
Notes			

Friday | 17 October 2025 - Waning Crescent

6:00		Today's quick wins	
7:00			
8:00			
9:00			
10:00			
11:00		Health and nutrition	
12:00			
13:00			
14:00		Today, I am grateful for…	
15:00			
16:00			
17:00		Today's self care	
18:00			
19:00			
20:00		Chart your cycle	
21:00			
22:00			
23:00		Positive affirmation	
Notes			

Saturday | 18 October 2025 - Waning Crescent

6:00	Today's quick wins
7:00	
8:00	
9:00	
10:00	
11:00	Health and nutrition
12:00	
13:00	
14:00	Today, I am grateful for…
15:00	
16:00	
17:00	Today's self care
18:00	
19:00	
20:00	Chart your cycle
21:00	
22:00	
23:00	Positive affirmation
Notes	

Sunday | 19 October 2025 - Waning Crescent

6:00	Today's quick wins
7:00	
8:00	
9:00	
10:00	
11:00	Health and nutrition
12:00	
13:00	
14:00	Today, I am grateful for...
15:00	
16:00	
17:00	Today's self care
18:00	
19:00	
20:00	Chart your cycle
21:00	
22:00	
23:00	Positive affirmation
Notes	

Monday | 20 October 2025 - Waning Crescent

6:00	Today's quick wins	
7:00		
8:00		
9:00		
10:00		
11:00	Health and nutrition	
12:00		
13:00		
14:00	Today, I am grateful for...	
15:00		
16:00		
17:00	Today's self care	
18:00		
19:00		
20:00	Chart your cycle	
21:00		
22:00		
23:00	Positive affirmation	
Notes		

Tuesday | 21 October 2025 - New Moon in Libra 12:24 GMT into Scorpio at 15.42

6:00		Today's quick wins	
7:00			
8:00			
9:00			
10:00			
11:00		Health and nutrition	
12:00			
13:00			
14:00		Today, I am grateful for…	
15:00			
16:00			
17:00		Today's self care	
18:00			
19:00			
20:00		Chart your cycle	
21:00			
22:00			
23:00		Positive affirmation	
Notes			

Wednesday | 22 October 2025 - Waxing Crescent

6:00		Today's quick wins	
7:00			
8:00			
9:00			
10:00			
11:00		Health and nutrition	
12:00			
13:00			
14:00		Today, I am grateful for…	
15:00			
16:00			
17:00		Today's self care	
18:00			
19:00			
20:00		Chart your cycle	
21:00			
22:00			
23:00		Positive affirmation	
Notes			

Thursday | 23 October 2025 - Waxing Crescent

6:00		Today's quick wins	
7:00			
8:00			
9:00			
10:00			
11:00		Health and nutrition	
12:00			
13:00			
14:00		Today, I am grateful for…	
15:00			
16:00			
17:00		Today's self care	
18:00			
19:00			
20:00		Chart your cycle	
21:00			
22:00			
23:00		Positive affirmation	
Notes			

Friday | 24 October 2025 - Waxing Crescent

6:00	Today's quick wins
7:00	
8:00	
9:00	
10:00	
11:00	Health and nutrition
12:00	
13:00	
14:00	Today, I am grateful for…
15:00	
16:00	
17:00	Today's self care
18:00	
19:00	
20:00	Chart your cycle
21:00	
22:00	
23:00	Positive affirmation
Notes	

Saturday | 25 October - Waxing Crescent

6:00	**Today's quick wins**
7:00	
8:00	
9:00	
10:00	
11:00	**Health and nutrition**
12:00	
13:00	
14:00	**Today, I am grateful for...**
15:00	
16:00	
17:00	**Today's self care**
18:00	
19:00	
20:00	**Chart your cycle**
21:00	
22:00	
23:00	**Positive affirmation**
Notes	

Sunday | 26 October 2025 - Waxing Crescent

6:00		Today's quick wins
7:00		
8:00		
9:00		
10:00		
11:00		Health and nutrition
12:00		
13:00		
14:00		Today, I am grateful for...
15:00		
16:00		
17:00		Today's self care
18:00		
19:00		
20:00		Chart your cycle
21:00		
22:00		
23:00		Positive affirmation
Notes		

Monday | 27 October 2025 - Waxing Crescent

6:00	Today's quick wins	
7:00		
8:00		
9:00		
10:00		
11:00	Health and nutrition	
12:00		
13:00		
14:00	Today, I am grateful for…	
15:00		
16:00		
17:00	Today's self care	
18:00		
19:00		
20:00	Chart your cycle	
21:00		
22:00		
23:00	Positive affirmation	
Notes		

Tuesday 28 October 2025 - Waxing Crescent

6:00		Today's quick wins
7:00		
8:00		
9:00		
10:00		
11:00		Health and nutrition
12:00		
13:00		
14:00		Today, I am grateful for…
15:00		
16:00		
17:00		Today's self care
18:00		
19:00		
20:00		Chart your cycle
21:00		
22:00		
23:00		Positive affirmation
Notes		

Wednesday | 29 October 2025 - First Quarter

6:00	Today's quick wins
7:00	
8:00	
9:00	
10:00	
11:00	Health and nutrition
12:00	
13:00	
14:00	Today, I am grateful for…
15:00	
16:00	
17:00	Today's self care
18:00	
19:00	
20:00	Chart your cycle
21:00	
22:00	
23:00	Positive affirmation
Notes	

Thursday | 30 October 2025 - Waxing Gibbous

6:00		Today's quick wins
7:00		
8:00		
9:00		
10:00		
11:00		Health and nutrition
12:00		
13:00		
14:00		Today, I am grateful for...
15:00		
16:00		
17:00		Today's self care
18:00		
19:00		
20:00		Chart your cycle
21:00		
22:00		
23:00		Positive affirmation
Notes		

Friday | 31 October 2025 - Waxing Gibbous

6:00		Today's quick wins	
7:00			
8:00			
9:00			
10:00			
11:00		Health and nutrition	
12:00			
13:00			
14:00		Today, I am grateful for…	
15:00			
16:00			
17:00		Today's self care	
18:00			
19:00			
20:00		Chart your cycle	
21:00			
22:00			
23:00		Positive affirmation	
Notes			

October achievements

Be proud of yourself and all that you have achieved this month. Write down your wins, big and small. If you have not achieved everything that you set out to do, that's okay! We learn and grow through our mistakes and experiences. You can use this space to make notes about anything that you have learned.

November 2025

Notes	Monday	Tuesday	Wednesday
	27	28	29
	3	4	5 ○
	10	11	12 ☽
	17	18	19
	24	25	26

Thursday	Friday	Saturday	Sunday
30	31	1	2
6	7	8	9
13	14	15	16
20 ●	21	22	23
27	28 ◐	29	30

November
Goddess Ma'at

MA'AT

Goddess of Balance, Truth, Law and Justice

Ma'at features heavily in the Egyptian book of the dead. The heart of the deceased is weighed on scales balanced with Ma'at's feather. Those with a light pure heart will journey into the afterlife. The 42 principles of Ma'at are said to be what the ten commandments are based on.

Ma'at is a continuous reminder to keep our hearts light with gratitude and kindness for earth and all her creatures.

When we grieve the injustices of the world we can look to Ma'at, her protective wings and balancing scales inspire us to create peace, harmony and balance within our own lives. This will ripple out into the world to create the future we want to pass on.

Book: Inroduction to Maat Philosophy: Introduction to Maat Philosophy: Ancient Egyptian Ethics & Metaphysics by Muata Ashby
Song: Rising Sun by Egyptian Meditation Temple
Moon phase: New moon
Crystal: Lapis Lazuli

My November Vision

"Whatever our individual troubles and challenges may be, it's important to pause every now and then to appreciate all that we have, on every level. We need to literally 'count our blessings,' give thanks for them, allow ourselves to enjoy them, and relish the experience of prosperity we already have."

Shakti Gawain

Saturday | 1 November 2025 - Waxing Gibbous

6:00	**Today's quick wins**
7:00	
8:00	
9:00	
10:00	
11:00	**Health and nutrition**
12:00	
13:00	
14:00	**Today, I am grateful for...**
15:00	
16:00	
17:00	**Today's self care**
18:00	
19:00	
20:00	**Chart your cycle**
21:00	
22:00	
23:00	**Positive affirmation**
Notes	

Sunday | 2 November 2025 - Waxing Gibbous

6:00	**Today's quick wins**
7:00	
8:00	
9:00	
10:00	
11:00	**Health and nutrition**
12:00	
13:00	
14:00	**Today, I am grateful for...**
15:00	
16:00	
17:00	**Today's self care**
18:00	
19:00	
20:00	**Chart your cycle**
21:00	
22:00	
23:00	**Positive affirmation**
Notes	

Monday | 3 November 2025 - Waxing Gibbous

6:00	Today's quick wins
7:00	
8:00	
9:00	
10:00	
11:00	Health and nutrition
12:00	
13:00	
14:00	Today, I am grateful for…
15:00	
16:00	
17:00	Today's self care
18:00	
19:00	
20:00	Chart your cycle
21:00	
22:00	
23:00	Positive affirmation
Notes	

Tuesday | 4 November 2025 - Waxing Gibbous

6:00	**Today's quick wins**
7:00	
8:00	
9:00	
10:00	
11:00	**Health and nutrition**
12:00	
13:00	
14:00	**Today, I am grateful for...**
15:00	
16:00	
17:00	**Today's self care**
18:00	
19:00	
20:00	**Chart your cycle**
21:00	
22:00	
23:00	**Positive affirmation**
Notes	

Wednesday | 5 November 2025 - Full Moon in Taurus 13:19 GMT

6:00	Today's quick wins	
7:00		
8:00		
9:00		
10:00		
11:00	Health and nutrition	
12:00		
13:00		
14:00	Today, I am grateful for…	
15:00		
16:00		
17:00	Today's self care	
18:00		
19:00		
20:00	Chart your cycle	
21:00		
22:00		
23:00	Positive affirmation	
Notes		

Thursday | 6 November 2025 - Waning Gibbous

6:00	Today's quick wins
7:00	
8:00	
9:00	
10:00	
11:00	Health and nutrition
12:00	
13:00	
14:00	Today, I am grateful for…
15:00	
16:00	
17:00	Today's self care
18:00	
19:00	
20:00	Chart your cycle
21:00	
22:00	
23:00	Positive affirmation
Notes	

Friday | 7 November 2025 - Waning Gibbous

6:00	**Today's quick wins**
7:00	
8:00	
9:00	
10:00	
11:00	**Health and nutrition**
12:00	
13:00	
14:00	**Today, I am grateful for...**
15:00	
16:00	
17:00	**Today's self care**
18:00	
19:00	
20:00	**Chart your cycle**
21:00	
22:00	
23:00	**Positive affirmation**
Notes	

Saturday | 8 November - Waning Gibbous

6:00	Today's quick wins	
7:00		
8:00		
9:00		
10:00		
11:00	Health and nutrition	
12:00		
13:00		
14:00	Today, I am grateful for...	
15:00		
16:00		
17:00	Today's self care	
18:00		
19:00		
20:00	Chart your cycle	
21:00		
22:00		
23:00	Positive affirmation	
Notes		

Sunday | 9 November 2025 - Waning Gibbous

6:00	**Today's quick wins**
7:00	
8:00	
9:00	
10:00	
11:00	**Health and nutrition**
12:00	
13:00	
14:00	**Today, I am grateful for...**
15:00	
16:00	
17:00	**Today's self care**
18:00	
19:00	
20:00	**Chart your cycle**
21:00	
22:00	
23:00	**Positive affirmation**
Notes	

Monday | 10 November 2025 - Waning Gibbous

6:00		Today's quick wins	
7:00			
8:00			
9:00			
10:00			
11:00		Health and nutrition	
12:00			
13:00			
14:00		Today, I am grateful for...	
15:00			
16:00			
17:00		Today's self care	
18:00			
19:00			
20:00		Chart your cycle	
21:00			
22:00			
23:00		Positive affirmation	
Notes			

Tuesday | 11 November 2025 - Waning Gibbous

6:00		**Today's quick wins**	
7:00			
8:00			
9:00			
10:00			
11:00		**Health and nutrition**	
12:00			
13:00			
14:00		**Today, I am grateful for…**	
15:00			
16:00			
17:00		**Today's self care**	
18:00			
19:00			
20:00		**Chart your cycle**	
21:00			
22:00			
23:00		**Positive affirmation**	
Notes			

Wednesday | 12 November 2025 - Last Quarter

6:00		Today's quick wins
7:00		
8:00		
9:00		
10:00		
11:00		Health and nutrition
12:00		
13:00		
14:00		Today, I am grateful for…
15:00		
16:00		
17:00		Today's self care
18:00		
19:00		
20:00		Chart your cycle
21:00		
22:00		
23:00		Positive affirmation
Notes		

Thursday | 13 November 2025 - Waning Crescent

6:00	**Today's quick wins**
7:00	
8:00	
9:00	
10:00	
11:00	**Health and nutrition**
12:00	
13:00	
14:00	**Today, I am grateful for...**
15:00	
16:00	
17:00	**Today's self care**
18:00	
19:00	
20:00	**Chart your cycle**
21:00	
22:00	
23:00	**Positive affirmation**
Notes	

Friday | 14 November 2025 - Waning Crescent

6:00		Today's quick wins	
7:00			
8:00			
9:00			
10:00			
11:00		Health and nutrition	
12:00			
13:00			
14:00		Today, I am grateful for...	
15:00			
16:00			
17:00		Today's self care	
18:00			
19:00			
20:00		Chart your cycle	
21:00			
22:00			
23:00		Positive affirmation	
Notes			

Saturday | 15 November 2025 - Waning Crescent

6:00	Today's quick wins
7:00	
8:00	
9:00	
10:00	
11:00	Health and nutrition
12:00	
13:00	
14:00	Today, I am grateful for...
15:00	
16:00	
17:00	Today's self care
18:00	
19:00	
20:00	Chart your cycle
21:00	
22:00	
23:00	Positive affirmation
Notes	

Sunday | 16 November 2025 - Waning Crescent

6:00		Today's quick wins
7:00		
8:00		
9:00		
10:00		
11:00		Health and nutrition
12:00		
13:00		
14:00		Today, I am grateful for…
15:00		
16:00		
17:00		Today's self care
18:00		
19:00		
20:00		Chart your cycle
21:00		
22:00		
23:00		Positive affirmation
Notes		

Monday | 17 November 2025 - Waning Crescent

6:00	Today's quick wins	
7:00		
8:00		
9:00		
10:00		
11:00	Health and nutrition	
12:00		
13:00		
14:00	Today, I am grateful for…	
15:00		
16:00		
17:00	Today's self care	
18:00		
19:00		
20:00	Chart your cycle	
21:00		
22:00		
23:00	Positive affirmation	
Notes		

Tuesday | 18 November 2025 - Waning Crescent

6:00		Today's quick wins
7:00		
8:00		
9:00		
10:00		
11:00		Health and nutrition
12:00		
13:00		
14:00		Today, I am grateful for...
15:00		
16:00		
17:00		Today's self care
18:00		
19:00		
20:00		Chart your cycle
21:00		
22:00		
23:00		Positive affirmation
Notes		

Wednesday | 19 November 2025 - Waning Crescent

6:00	Today's quick wins	
7:00		
8:00		
9:00		
10:00		
11:00	Health and nutrition	
12:00		
13:00		
14:00	Today, I am grateful for…	
15:00		
16:00		
17:00	Today's self care	
18:00		
19:00		
20:00	Chart your cycle	
21:00		
22:00		
23:00	Positive affirmation	
Notes		

Thursday | 20 November 2025 - New Moon in Scorpio
06:46 GMT into Sagittarius at 10.26

6:00	Today's quick wins
7:00	
8:00	
9:00	
10:00	
11:00	Health and nutrition
12:00	
13:00	
14:00	Today, I am grateful for…
15:00	
16:00	
17:00	Today's self care
18:00	
19:00	
20:00	Chart your cycle
21:00	
22:00	
23:00	Positive affirmation
Notes	

Friday | 21 November 2025 - Waxing Crescent

6:00		Today's quick wins	
7:00			
8:00			
9:00			
10:00			
11:00		Health and nutrition	
12:00			
13:00			
14:00		Today, I am grateful for...	
15:00			
16:00			
17:00		Today's self care	
18:00			
19:00			
20:00		Chart your cycle	
21:00			
22:00			
23:00		Positive affirmation	
Notes			

Saturday | 22 November 2025 - Waxing Crescent

6:00	**Today's quick wins**
7:00	
8:00	
9:00	
10:00	
11:00	**Health and nutrition**
12:00	
13:00	
14:00	**Today, I am grateful for...**
15:00	
16:00	
17:00	**Today's self care**
18:00	
19:00	
20:00	**Chart your cycle**
21:00	
22:00	
23:00	**Positive affirmation**
Notes	

Sunday | 23 November - Waxing Crescent

6:00		Today's quick wins	
7:00			
8:00			
9:00			
10:00			
11:00		Health and nutrition	
12:00			
13:00			
14:00		Today, I am grateful for…	
15:00			
16:00			
17:00		Today's self care	
18:00			
19:00			
20:00		Chart your cycle	
21:00			
22:00			
23:00		Positive affirmation	
Notes			

Monday | 24 November 2025 - Waxing Crescent

6:00	Today's quick wins	
7:00		
8:00		
9:00		
10:00		
11:00	Health and nutrition	
12:00		
13:00		
14:00	Today, I am grateful for...	
15:00		
16:00		
17:00	Today's self care	
18:00		
19:00		
20:00	Chart your cycle	
21:00		
22:00		
23:00	Positive affirmation	
Notes		

Tuesday | 25 November 2025 - Waxing Crescent

6:00	Today's quick wins	
7:00		
8:00		
9:00		
10:00		
11:00	Health and nutrition	
12:00		
13:00		
14:00	Today, I am grateful for…	
15:00		
16:00		
17:00	Today's self care	
18:00		
19:00		
20:00	Chart your cycle	
21:00		
22:00		
23:00	Positive affirmation	
Notes		

Wednesday | 26 November 2025 - Waxing Crescent

6:00	Today's quick wins
7:00	
8:00	
9:00	
10:00	
11:00	Health and nutrition
12:00	
13:00	
14:00	Today, I am grateful for...
15:00	
16:00	
17:00	Today's self care
18:00	
19:00	
20:00	Chart your cycle
21:00	
22:00	
23:00	Positive affirmation
Notes	

Thursday | 27 November 2025 - Waxing Crescent

6:00		Today's quick wins
7:00		
8:00		
9:00		
10:00		
11:00		Health and nutrition
12:00		
13:00		
14:00		Today, I am grateful for…
15:00		
16:00		
17:00		Today's self care
18:00		
19:00		
20:00		Chart your cycle
21:00		
22:00		
23:00		Positive affirmation
Notes		

Friday | 28 November 2025 - First Quarter

6:00	Today's quick wins
7:00	
8:00	
9:00	
10:00	
11:00	Health and nutrition
12:00	
13:00	
14:00	Today, I am grateful for...
15:00	
16:00	
17:00	Today's self care
18:00	
19:00	
20:00	Chart your cycle
21:00	
22:00	
23:00	Positive affirmation
Notes	

Saturday | 29 November 2025 - Waxing Gibbous

6:00		Today's quick wins	
7:00			
8:00			
9:00			
10:00			
11:00		Health and nutrition	
12:00			
13:00			
14:00		Today, I am grateful for…	
15:00			
16:00			
17:00		Today's self care	
18:00			
19:00			
20:00		Chart your cycle	
21:00			
22:00			
23:00		Positive affirmation	
Notes			

Sunday | 30 November 2025 - Waxing Gibbous

6:00		Today's quick wins
7:00		
8:00		
9:00		
10:00		
11:00		Health and nutrition
12:00		
13:00		
14:00		Today, I am grateful for...
15:00		
16:00		
17:00		Today's self care
18:00		
19:00		
20:00		Chart your cycle
21:00		
22:00		
23:00		Positive affirmation
Notes		

November achievements

Be proud of yourself and all that you have achieved this month. Write down your wins, big and small. If you have not achieved everything that you set out to do, that's okay! We learn and grow through our mistakes and experiences. You can use this space to make notes about anything that you have learned.

December 2025

Notes	Monday	Tuesday	Wednesday
	1	2	3
	8	9	10
	15	16	17
	22	23	24
	29	30	31

Thursday	Friday	Saturday	Sunday
4 ○	5	6	7
11 ☽	12	13	14
18	19	20 ●	21 *Winter Solstice*
25	26	27 ☾	28

December
Goddess Annapurna

ANNAPURNA

Goddess of Food and Nourishment.

An avatar of goddess Parvati who represents spiritual femininity, the yin to her husband Shiva's yang. The couple once got into an argument about life when Shiva claimed life is nothing but an illusion. Parvati who had created the world, felt betrayed and disappeared - which caused famines and starvation on earth.

She could not stand to see the suffering, so she returned to earth under an avatar of goddess Annapurna where she opened a kitchen and gave out food. Shiva was humbled and realised how much he too needed his wife.

In our fast paced society we often sit to eat without giving thanks. It is worth taking time to think about those who have worked to bring food to our plates; nature, farmers, drivers, shop workers... When we have reverence for our meal our food seems to hold extra nourishment for mind, body and soul.

Book: Sacred Seed by Global Peace Initiative of Women
Song: Annapurna by LaYam
Moon phase: Full moon
Crystal: Jade

My Vision for December

Monday | 1 December 2025 - Waxing Gibbous

6:00	Today's quick wins
7:00	
8:00	
9:00	
10:00	
11:00	Health and nutrition
12:00	
13:00	
14:00	Today, I am grateful for...
15:00	
16:00	
17:00	Today's self care
18:00	
19:00	
20:00	Chart your cycle
21:00	
22:00	
23:00	Positive affirmation
Notes	

Tuesday | 2 December 2025 - Waxing Gibbous

6:00	Today's quick wins	
7:00		
8:00		
9:00		
10:00		
11:00	Health and nutrition	
12:00		
13:00		
14:00	Today, I am grateful for…	
15:00		
16:00		
17:00	Today's self care	
18:00		
19:00		
20:00	Chart your cycle	
21:00		
22:00		
23:00	Positive affirmation	
Notes		

Wednesday | 3 December 2025 - Waxing Gibbous

6:00	Today's quick wins	
7:00		
8:00		
9:00		
10:00		
11:00	Health and nutrition	
12:00		
13:00		
14:00	Today, I am grateful for...	
15:00		
16:00		
17:00	Today's self care	
18:00		
19:00		
20:00	Chart your cycle	
21:00		
22:00		
23:00	Positive affirmation	
Notes		

Thursday | 4 December 2025 - Full Moon in Gemini 23:13 GMT

6:00	Today's quick wins
7:00	
8:00	
9:00	
10:00	
11:00	Health and nutrition
12:00	
13:00	
14:00	Today, I am grateful for...
15:00	
16:00	
17:00	Today's self care
18:00	
19:00	
20:00	Chart your cycle
21:00	
22:00	
23:00	Positive affirmation
Notes	

Friday | 5 December 2025 - Waning Gibbous

6:00	Today's quick wins	
7:00		
8:00		
9:00		
10:00		
11:00	Health and nutrition	
12:00		
13:00		
14:00	Today, I am grateful for...	
15:00		
16:00		
17:00	Today's self care	
18:00		
19:00		
20:00	Chart your cycle	
21:00		
22:00		
23:00	Positive affirmation	
Notes		

Saturday | 6 December 2025 - Waning Gibbous

6:00	**Today's quick wins**
7:00	
8:00	
9:00	
10:00	
11:00	**Health and nutrition**
12:00	
13:00	
14:00	**Today, I am grateful for...**
15:00	
16:00	
17:00	**Today's self care**
18:00	
19:00	
20:00	**Chart your cycle**
21:00	
22:00	
23:00	**Positive affirmation**
Notes	

Sunday | 7 December 2025 - Waning Gibbous

6:00		Today's quick wins
7:00		
8:00		
9:00		
10:00		
11:00		Health and nutrition
12:00		
13:00		
14:00		Today, I am grateful for...
15:00		
16:00		
17:00		Today's self care
18:00		
19:00		
20:00		Chart your cycle
21:00		
22:00		
23:00		Positive affirmation
Notes		

Monday | 8 December - Waning Gibbous

6:00	**Today's quick wins**
7:00	
8:00	
9:00	
10:00	
11:00	**Health and nutrition**
12:00	
13:00	
14:00	**Today, I am grateful for...**
15:00	
16:00	
17:00	**Today's self care**
18:00	
19:00	
20:00	**Chart your cycle**
21:00	
22:00	
23:00	**Positive affirmation**
Notes	

Tuesday | 9 December 2025 - Waning Gibbous

6:00	Today's quick wins
7:00	
8:00	
9:00	
10:00	
11:00	Health and nutrition
12:00	
13:00	
14:00	Today, I am grateful for...
15:00	
16:00	
17:00	Today's self care
18:00	
19:00	
20:00	Chart your cycle
21:00	
22:00	
23:00	Positive affirmation
Notes	

Wednesday | 10 December 2025 - Waning Gibbous

6:00		Today's quick wins	
7:00			
8:00			
9:00			
10:00			
11:00		Health and nutrition	
12:00			
13:00			
14:00		Today, I am grateful for...	
15:00			
16:00			
17:00		Today's self care	
18:00			
19:00			
20:00		Chart your cycle	
21:00			
22:00			
23:00		Positive affirmation	
Notes			

Thursday | 11 December 2025 - Last Quarter

6:00	**Today's quick wins**
7:00	
8:00	
9:00	
10:00	
11:00	**Health and nutrition**
12:00	
13:00	
14:00	**Today, I am grateful for...**
15:00	
16:00	
17:00	**Today's self care**
18:00	
19:00	
20:00	**Chart your cycle**
21:00	
22:00	
23:00	**Positive affirmation**
Notes	

Friday | 12 December 2025 - Waning Crescent

6:00	**Today's quick wins**
7:00	
8:00	
9:00	
10:00	
11:00	**Health and nutrition**
12:00	
13:00	
14:00	**Today, I am grateful for...**
15:00	
16:00	
17:00	**Today's self care**
18:00	
19:00	
20:00	**Chart your cycle**
21:00	
22:00	
23:00	**Positive affirmation**

Notes

Saturday | 13 December 2025 - Waning Crescent

6:00		Today's quick wins	
7:00			
8:00			
9:00			
10:00			
11:00		Health and nutrition	
12:00			
13:00			
14:00		Today, I am grateful for...	
15:00			
16:00			
17:00		Today's self care	
18:00			
19:00			
20:00		Chart your cycle	
21:00			
22:00			
23:00		Positive affirmation	
Notes			

Sunday | 14 December 2025 - Waning Crescent

6:00	**Today's quick wins**
7:00	
8:00	
9:00	
10:00	
11:00	**Health and nutrition**
12:00	
13:00	
14:00	**Today, I am grateful for…**
15:00	
16:00	
17:00	**Today's self care**
18:00	
19:00	
20:00	**Chart your cycle**
21:00	
22:00	
23:00	**Positive affirmation**
Notes	

Monday | 15 December 2025 - Waning Crescent

6:00	Today's quick wins
7:00	
8:00	
9:00	
10:00	
11:00	Health and nutrition
12:00	
13:00	
14:00	Today, I am grateful for…
15:00	
16:00	
17:00	Today's self care
18:00	
19:00	
20:00	Chart your cycle
21:00	
22:00	
23:00	Positive affirmation
Notes	

Tuesday | 16 December 2025 - Waning Crescent

6:00		Today's quick wins	
7:00			
8:00			
9:00			
10:00			
11:00		Health and nutrition	
12:00			
13:00			
14:00		Today, I am grateful for...	
15:00			
16:00			
17:00		Today's self care	
18:00			
19:00			
20:00		Chart your cycle	
21:00			
22:00			
23:00		Positive affirmation	
Notes			

# Wednesday | 17 December 2025 - Waning Crescent

6:00		Today's quick wins	
7:00			
8:00			
9:00			
10:00			
11:00		Health and nutrition	
12:00			
13:00			
14:00		Today, I am grateful for…	
15:00			
16:00			
17:00		Today's self care	
18:00			
19:00			
20:00		Chart your cycle	
21:00			
22:00			
23:00		Positive affirmation	
Notes			

Thursday | 18 December 2025 - Waning Crescent

6:00	Today's quick wins
7:00	
8:00	
9:00	
10:00	
11:00	Health and nutrition
12:00	
13:00	
14:00	Today, I am grateful for…
15:00	
16:00	
17:00	Today's self care
18:00	
19:00	
20:00	Chart your cycle
21:00	
22:00	
23:00	Positive affirmation
Notes	

Friday | 19 December 2025 - Waning Crescent

6:00		Today's quick wins
7:00		
8:00		
9:00		
10:00		
11:00		Health and nutrition
12:00		
13:00		
14:00		Today, I am grateful for...
15:00		
16:00		
17:00		Today's self care
18:00		
19:00		
20:00		Chart your cycle
21:00		
22:00		
23:00		Positive affirmation
Notes		

Saturday | 20 December 2025 - New Moon in Sagittarius
01:43 GMT into Capricorn at 04.53

6:00	Today's quick wins
7:00	
8:00	
9:00	
10:00	
11:00	Health and nutrition
12:00	
13:00	
14:00	Today, I am grateful for...
15:00	
16:00	
17:00	Today's self care
18:00	
19:00	
20:00	Chart your cycle
21:00	
22:00	
23:00	Positive affirmation
Notes	

Sunday | 21 December 2025 - Waxing Crescent
Winter Solstice

6:00	Today's quick wins	
7:00		
8:00		
9:00		
10:00		
11:00	Health and nutrition	
12:00		
13:00		
14:00	Today, I am grateful for...	
15:00		
16:00		
17:00	Today's self care	
18:00		
19:00		
20:00	Chart your cycle	
21:00		
22:00		
23:00	Positive affirmation	
Notes		

Monday | 22 December 2025 - Waxing Crescent

6:00	Today's quick wins	
7:00		
8:00		
9:00		
10:00		
11:00	Health and nutrition	
12:00		
13:00		
14:00	Today, I am grateful for…	
15:00		
16:00		
17:00	Today's self care	
18:00		
19:00		
20:00	Chart your cycle	
21:00		
22:00		
23:00	Positive affirmation	
Notes		

Tuesday 23 December - Waxing Crescent

6:00	Today's quick wins
7:00	
8:00	
9:00	
10:00	
11:00	Health and nutrition
12:00	
13:00	
14:00	Today, I am grateful for...
15:00	
16:00	
17:00	Today's self care
18:00	
19:00	
20:00	Chart your cycle
21:00	
22:00	
23:00	Positive affirmation
Notes	

Wednesday | 24 December 2025 - Waxing Crescent

6:00	**Today's quick wins**
7:00	
8:00	
9:00	
10:00	
11:00	**Health and nutrition**
12:00	
13:00	
14:00	**Today, I am grateful for...**
15:00	
16:00	
17:00	**Today's self care**
18:00	
19:00	
20:00	**Chart your cycle**
21:00	
22:00	
23:00	**Positive affirmation**
Notes	

Thursday | 25 December 2025 - Waxing Crescent

6:00	**Today's quick wins**
7:00	
8:00	
9:00	
10:00	
11:00	**Health and nutrition**
12:00	
13:00	
14:00	**Today, I am grateful for...**
15:00	
16:00	
17:00	**Today's self care**
18:00	
19:00	
20:00	**Chart your cycle**
21:00	
22:00	
23:00	**Positive affirmation**
Notes	

Friday | 26 December 2025 - Waxing Crescent

6:00	Today's quick wins	
7:00		
8:00		
9:00		
10:00		
11:00	Health and nutrition	
12:00		
13:00		
14:00	Today, I am grateful for...	
15:00		
16:00		
17:00	Today's self care	
18:00		
19:00		
20:00	Chart your cycle	
21:00		
22:00		
23:00	Positive affirmation	
Notes		

Saturday | 27 December 2025 - First Quarter

6:00		Today's quick wins
7:00		
8:00		
9:00		
10:00		
11:00		Health and nutrition
12:00		
13:00		
14:00		Today, I am grateful for…
15:00		
16:00		
17:00		Today's self care
18:00		
19:00		
20:00		Chart your cycle
21:00		
22:00		
23:00		Positive affirmation
Notes		

Sunday | 28 December 2025 - Waxing Gibbous

6:00		Today's quick wins
7:00		
8:00		
9:00		
10:00		
11:00		Health and nutrition
12:00		
13:00		
14:00		Today, I am grateful for...
15:00		
16:00		
17:00		Today's self care
18:00		
19:00		
20:00		Chart your cycle
21:00		
22:00		
23:00		Positive affirmation
Notes		

Monday | 29 December 2025 - Waxing Gibbous

6:00		Today's quick wins	
7:00			
8:00			
9:00			
10:00			
11:00		Health and nutrition	
12:00			
13:00			
14:00		Today, I am grateful for...	
15:00			
16:00			
17:00		Today's self care	
18:00			
19:00			
20:00		Chart your cycle	
21:00			
22:00			
23:00		Positive affirmation	
Notes			

Tuesday | 30 December 2025 - Waxing Gibbous

6:00	**Today's quick wins**
7:00	
8:00	
9:00	
10:00	
11:00	**Health and nutrition**
12:00	
13:00	
14:00	**Today, I am grateful for...**
15:00	
16:00	
17:00	**Today's self care**
18:00	
19:00	
20:00	**Chart your cycle**
21:00	
22:00	
23:00	**Positive affirmation**
Notes	

Wednesday | 31 December 2025 - Waxing Gibbous

6:00		Today's quick wins	
7:00			
8:00			
9:00			
10:00			
11:00		Health and nutrition	
12:00			
13:00			
14:00		Today, I am grateful for…	
15:00			
16:00			
17:00		Today's self care	
18:00			
19:00			
20:00		Chart your cycle	
21:00			
22:00			
23:00		Positive affirmation	
Notes			

December achievements

Be proud of yourself and all that you have achieved this month. Write down your wins, big and small. If you have not achieved everything that you set out to do, that's okay! We learn and grow through our mistakes and experiences. You can use this space to make notes about anything that you have learned.

What have I achieved and how have I grown in 2025...

My 2025 Reading List

Film & Podcast Notes

Notes

Notes

Notes

Vision for 2026

www.ingramcontent.com/pod-product-compliance
Lightning Source LLC
Chambersburg PA
CBHW072149200426
43209CB00051B/991